KIM-JOY
ORDINARY JOY

A REALISTIC GUIDE TO BEING YOURSELF

This book is a work of non-fiction based on the life, experiences and recollections of the author. In some cases names of people, places, dates, sequences and the detail of events have been changed to protect the privacy of others.

Quadrille, Penguin Random House UK,
One Embassy Gardens, 8 Viaduct Gardens,
London SW11 7BW

Quadrille Publishing Limited is part of the Penguin Random House group of companies whose addresses can be found at global.penguinrandomhouse.com

Penguin Random House UK

Text © Kim-Joy 2025
Illustrations © Linda van den Berg 2025
Typography © Mary Kate McDevitt 2025
Design and layout © Quadrille 2025

Kim-Joy has asserted her right to be identified as the author of this Work in accordance with the Copyright, Designs and Patents Act 1988

No part of this book may be used or reproduced in any manner for the purpose of training artificial intelligence technologies or systems. In accordance with Article 4(3) of the DSM Directive 2019/790, Penguin Random House expressly reserves this work from the text and data mining exception.

Published by Quadrille in 2025

www.penguin.co.uk

A CIP catalogue record for this book is available from the British Library

ISBN 9781837831951

10 9 8 7 6 5 4 3 2 1

Managing Director: Sarah Lavelle
Editorial Director: Kate Pollard
Editor: Sofie Shearman
Co-writer: Tara O'Sullivan
Sensitivity Reader: Louise Chandler
Design Manager: Katherine Case
Design and Art Direction: Katy Everett
Illustrations: Linda van den Berg
Typography: Mary Kate McDevitt
Production Manager: Sabeena Atchia

The information in this book has been compiled as general guidance on the specific subjects addressed. It is not a substitute and not to be relied on for medical, healthcare or pharmaceutical professional advice. Please consult your GP before changing, stopping or starting any medical treatment. So far as the author is aware the information given is correct and up to date as at 28th April 2025. Practice, laws and regulations all change and the reader should obtain up to date professional advice on any such issues. The author and publishers disclaim, as far as the law allows, any liability arising directly or indirectly from the use or misuse of the information contained in this book.

Colour reproduction by p2d

Printed in China by RR Donnelley Asia Printing Solution Limited

The authorised representative in the EEA is Penguin Random House Ireland, Morrison Chambers, 32 Nassau Street, Dublin D02 YH68.

Penguin Random House is committed to a sustainable future for our business, our readers and our planet. This book is made from Forest Stewardship Council® certified paper.

MIX
Paper | Supporting responsible forestry
FSC® C018179

KIM-JOY
ORDINARY JOY

A REALISTIC GUIDE TO BEING YOURSELF

ILLUSTRATIONS BY LINDA VAN DEN BERG
LETTERING DESIGN BY MARY KATE McDEVIT

Quadrille

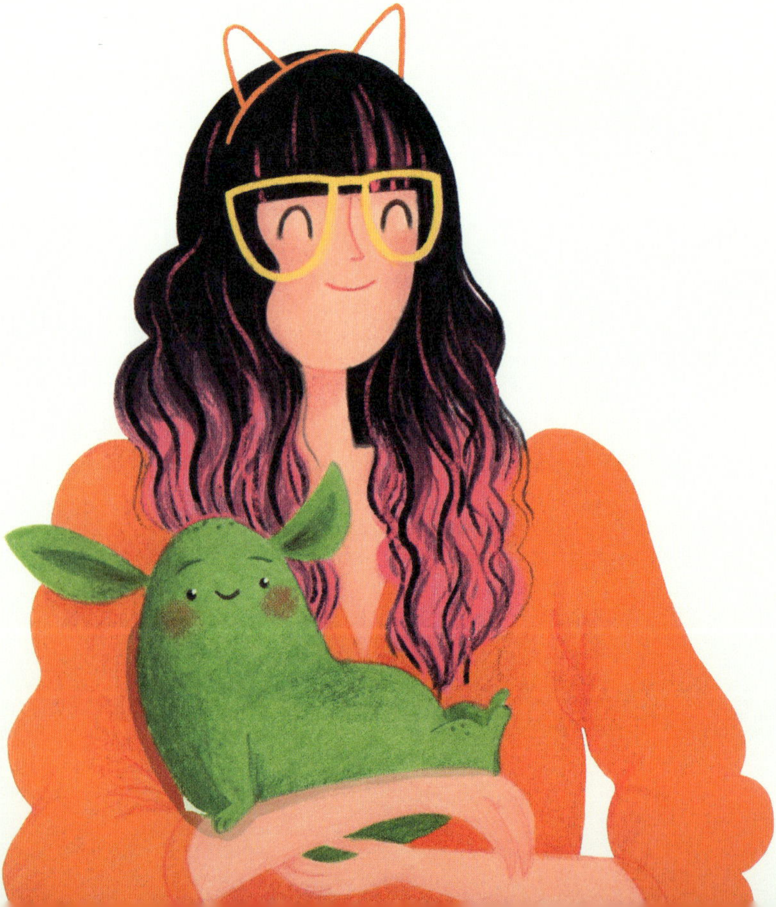

Contents

Introduction	6
Some people won't like you, and it's OK to say no	16
Finding the people and spaces that bring you calm and joy	42
'Fake it till you make it' and imposter phenomenon	64
Too quiet	80
Laziness doesn't exist	102
Vulnerability	128
Being childlike	150
I'd rather be kind than pretty	174
Understanding how other people think	198
Conclusion	214
Resources	221
Acknowledgements	223
About the author	224

Introduction

Joy is something I think about a lot. Perhaps that's partly because of my name – Kim-Joy – but I think it's also because I've spent a lot of my life struggling to feel safe and comfortable, and to me, feeling safe and comfortable is a big part of what joy is.

I enjoy the Chinese proverb 'There is no way to happiness; happiness is the way.' I take this to mean that happiness isn't something that takes a specific route; it isn't a destination, and it's not something that is attained in perpetuity. Instead, happiness is derived from everyday, ordinary things. It fluctuates daily. And it's something to treasure when you feel it. Ordinary joy: it's not always about big, life-changing moments. It's the small things, the little moments that make life feel that bit more magical. It's lighting a candle, putting on comfortable socks and baking a cake; but it's also making choices that are healthy for you, and saying no to the things that hurt you or make you feel less than. It's realizing who you are and what you want and need, and doing yourself the kindness of seeking out those things. In many ways, it's about authenticity; not trying to be somebody else, or fit in with others, or meet society's expectations. It's about meeting yourself where you are, being kind and compassionate with yourself and others, and, little by little, building a life that brings you peace and calm – and joy.

I often fall into the trap of thinking, **If only I can achieve x, then I'll be able to do y, and then I'll be happy.** But then y comes along, and I realize I'm *not* happy. This isn't to say that y is not a great accomplishment or something to be proud of – in fact, the likelihood is that y can bring a lot of everyday joy. But after a while, y isn't enough. The goalposts continue to stretch out further – because what about z? Z is just out of sight in the fog, but temptingly *there*... so just keeping pushing forward, and then you'll be happy finally, right? But no. It loops round to a, to b, to c...

I thought I'd be happy when I designed my perfect kitchen: pink and green, cozy, full of plants, with plenty of cupboards for all my baking bits and bobs, with every measurement calculated to create a flowing space – all exactly how I wanted it to be. And it does bring me a lot of joy every day. Almost every day, I tell my partner Nabil, 'I love my kitchen,' and then I ask him, 'Do you love your kitchen?' But there's always something more to do in the house, another mission, and so I keep chasing the joy, looking for that way to happiness, rather than understanding that **happiness *is* the way.**

All of this is to say that I'm not perfect. I make mistakes and get tricked by the happiness fallacy frequently. But I try to notice it when it happens. I take joy in my kitchen every day. Just opening one of the drawers makes me feel happy. Especially if I choose the drawer (now two drawers!) that's full of sprinkles.

But it's not just the material things. More importantly, it's the little moments, like seeing a cake rising in the oven, or feeling the tiles under my feet, which Nabil and I proudly laid all by ourselves! I take joy in the little imperfections in those tiles; three of them came without protective coating, for some reason, so they always look dirtier than the others. At first, I was disappointed. Now those three tiles just make me laugh inside. They're totally fine. They're kind of fun. I like to skip over them for amusement, like that game 'the floor is lava' you might've played as a kid.

Ordinary joy can also be found in things like saying 'hello' to a random stranger, or complimenting someone's outfit/hair/vibes. Making other people happy without expecting anything in return always makes me happy.

When I talk about 'joy', I'm not referring to feeling happy all the time – *I'm* definitely not happy all the time, even if I may seem it on the surface. Actually, **joy is about allowing yourself to feel every emotion**, and as mentioned previously, it is not a destination; it will ebb and flow.

Experiencing joy can be like the moment you see a flower emerge on an orchid. The next day, the orchid may drop a leaf – but then the next week, perhaps there's another flower. Joy is a collection of those short-lived blossoming moments, and it's interspersed among other, less leafy times. That's a good thing – because how can you know what joy is without experiencing the opposite? An orchid can't be forced to flower (in fact, it will definitely drop leaves if you overwater it, because it likes to really dry out in between drinks). In order to flower and thrive, an orchid needs to be nurtured intentionally, given small amounts of water, here and there. It takes patience and time.

There is no 'right way' to experience joy. The goal is messy, realistic, ordinary joy.

I'm not writing this book because I've got everything figured out. I'm writing this book because, like most of us (and probably you, as you've picked up this book), I've spent much of my life pretending to be what I'm not, and I've realized that the more I pretend, the further I get sucked into the doom spiral of feeling disconnected, losing all sense of who I am, and feeling a lack of joy. I'm making up for that now.

For many of us, childhood trauma, mental health issues and society all play a role here. Everyone's experience is different, and I can't speak to your own experiences, but I can take a moment to share my own.

My mum is Chinese, and grew up in Malaysia. She came to the UK to study, but was deported for working more hours than her visa allowed. She met my dad and ended up in Belgium. My dad was already married with two children. My mum then had three kids with him (me and two brothers, one younger and one older). It wasn't ideal. We moved to the UK when I was five years old, but my parents' marriage was always tumultuous and they divorced. My dad went to India and remarried. At the same time, my mum was struggling as a single mother on benefits taking care of three kids. Both my mum and my older brother have schizophrenia.

As a side note, I asked my mum if she was OK with me mentioning her schizophrenia in this book. At first, she said she'd rather not because of the stigma around it. But then she changed her mind and said, **'Why should it be something to hide?'**.

Lots of people don't really understand schizophrenia, confusing it with dissociative identity disorder (formerly known as multiple personality disorder), which is an entirely different condition. Schizophrenia is a complex mental illness and is deserving of understanding – just like any other mental illness.

So, in short, our home life was very challenging. Despite this, my mum did her best with what she was given. Just like all of us. We're all just doing our best with the difficult cards we're dealt. One of the best things my mum did was to always tell me to stay true to myself, never let myself feel small and to do what makes me happiest, whenever possible. I spent some time not listening to this advice, but gradually I changed, and realized she was right.

I was also lucky that my stepmum (my dad's ex-wife), who I grew up with in Belgium, became like a second mum. She has also been a strong role model for me – from the age of three she believed I would be a writer one day. She is never surprised when I tell her about the next book I'm working on. It's nice to have people believe in you.

When I started secondary school, I developed selective mutism (which I'll explain in more detail in chapter four), and continued to experience severe social anxiety long after that. This went largely unnoticed at home because there was so much going on, and because I could still speak and communicate there – just not at school. At school, I was the silent half-Chinese kid with no friends and no personality, while at home, I could talk and I could shout, but I would still feel alone and like I didn't belong or fit in.

Because of my difficulty fitting in and understanding who the 'real me' was, the subject of authenticity and figuring out life and other people has become a lifelong obsession. It's informed almost everything I've done, from what I've studied (sociology and psychology) to the jobs I've had (working in care homes, in an inpatient unit for people with learning disabilities, and in the community with people with anxiety and depression). I've figured out a lot about myself in the process, understanding my own people-pleasing tendencies, social anxiety, trauma and suspected autism, and all the things that make me 'me'. And along the way, I've found tough times and struggles; but also joy. Everyday, simple, ordinary joy.

Joy will look different for you compared to me: we all have different values, wants and needs, and we all have different options available to us. Throughout this book, I've shared my own stories and experiences, but I've also tried to be mindful of the varying lived experiences and challenges that you might face, that are different to my own. We all have different amounts of capital – be it social, cultural and/or financial – and this intersects with what we are able to do and change.

We all have a lot of differences. But I've always felt that what unifies us is our knowledge and sharing of our experiences. **Knowledge is power.** The more awareness we have of why we are the way we are, and how society forms barriers for us, the better equipped we are to see the holes. And then hopefully poke through those, allowing that bit of ordinary joy to peek through.

This book isn't about telling you what you should and must do, or making you feel bad for factors out of your control. Nor is it about telling you that I've got everything sorted (absolutely not) and that there are magical solutions to suddenly feel better. I've tried to stay as nuanced as possible.

I hope it's already clear, but I want to reiterate that I am by no means living a perfect life. I haven't got it all figured out. There is a lot in my life that I'm grateful and feel privileged for, including my home, my partner Nabil, my cats Inki and Mochi, my career and my community. But there are also things I'm still working on, and challenges I'm facing. For the last few years, I've been dealing with long-term health issues, including chronic daily migraine, that have completely upended my life. My world had to get a lot smaller, and my days had to get a lot slower. As someone who has always loved learning new things and getting things done, it's been hard having to slow down and stop. I've struggled with severe brain fog, reduced mobility and intense fatigue. I've spent hours in waiting rooms and hospitals seeing specialists, trying treatments, and attempting to figure out how to live with my condition. I've also spent time trying to understand my past trauma, my autism and my social anxiety. It's a bit of a rocky adventure, but I've learned a lot along the way, and I hope that by sharing it with you, I can help you with parts of your own adventure.

You might find that some parts of this book speak to you more than others; but overall I hope that there will be moments within these pages that bring you comfort and possibly bring about positive change.

This is an overview of the chapters of this book that I felt were most important for feeling **ordinary joy**:

- People-pleasing and learning to say no when you need to

- Finding your people and creating a space that makes you feel safe and secure

- Imposter phenomenon, and the ways in which societal expectations (and our own inner voices) can seem to sabotage us

- Quietness, and why there's nothing wrong with being different

- Rejecting the idea of laziness (it doesn't exist, and you deserve to rest!)

- Being vulnerable and connecting more fully with yourself and others

- Embracing your childlike tendencies and finding joy in little things

- The judgements we and others make about our physical appearance, and the importance of kindness

- Understanding how we think – and how other people think, too

I've roughly structured each chapter as follows:

- A story of my own experience relating to the chapter topic. (Hopefully it will make you think of your own experience!)

- Unpicking the story – what's going on? Why? Reflections and how you could relate this to your own experiences.

- Explanations, plus psychological and sociological theories around what's happening.

- What are the real-world challenges here (keeping it realistic)?

- What could be changed here/possible questions you could ask yourself as reflection points and ways to get a little more joy in your life. You could mull these over in your head, or write them down in a journal.

Then there are these weird guys too: our goblins! Because this book needs some fun – after all, it's about joy. And we all have an inner goblin eager for more joy.

So, let's begin.

KIM-JOY

1

Some people won't like you, and it's OK to say no

For some kids, the idea of going to a school fair would sound fun and exciting – games, sweets, fun with their friends. Then there are the kids whose nervous systems react to this like it's a bungee jump. For me, because of my social anxiety, I was firmly in the latter camp. On the day of my school fair, I'd spent the morning doing everything in my power to persuade my mum not to take me.

It didn't work.

When we got there, I walked awkwardly around, pretending to be interested in the stalls. A smiling lady at a table beckoned me over and asked me if I wanted to try. I shrunk inside, but agreeably moved closer.

It was a game. You had to put on a rubber washing-up glove, then stick your gloved hand through a hole into a box, and feel around to choose a mystery prize.

I said yes, because saying yes is the easiest option when you want to be liked. I was nervous as I put on the glove and reached into the box. As I pulled out my prize, eager to see what I'd retrieved, the smile on the lady's face disappeared, and her expression became stern.

The rubber glove had split.

And all I remember is her angrily telling me I'd broken it, over and over.

'You've broken the glove.'

'I can't believe you did that.'

'Look what you've done.'

*'Where am I going to get another one?
The game's ruined.'*

I stood there, my face hot, mumbling 'sorry' over and over. I was always deeply conscious of wanting to follow the rules and not do anything 'wrong', and now I had messed up. My stupid big clumsy hand had broken this glove, and I'd upset someone. This lady had liked me before, but now, I told myself, she'd realized the truth about me.

That I always disappoint.

> YOU'VE BROKEN THE GLOVE!

> I CAN'T BELIEVE YOU DID THAT.

> LOOK WHAT YOU'VE DONE.

> WHERE AM I GOING TO GET ANOTHER ONE? THE GAME'S RUINED.

> Sorry. Sorry. Sorry. Sorry. Sorry. Sorry.

When I was growing up, nothing terrified me more than the idea of being disapproved of, or disliked. I lived in fear of being told off or shouted at, of being told I wasn't good enough. More than anything, I wanted to be liked.

I must have been nine or ten that day at the school fair. On some level, I was old enough to know that her reaction was out of proportion to the situation – it was a rubber glove in a game at a school fair, after all – but that small shred of reason was miniscule compared to my feelings of guilt. I was overwhelmed, and could only stand there and think, **I always mess things up. I always disappoint people.**

So, why did I feel that way?

Why did it feel so terrible?

Negative core beliefs

When you're a newborn, you're yet to learn any negative core beliefs.

But throughout your childhood, those core beliefs start to develop. These can be formed in all sorts of ways, usually through regularly repeated messages that reinforce certain ideas. Some of them are positive; if you're repeatedly praised and recognized for being helpful, generous and empathetic, for example, you may, over time, develop the core belief that you're a kind person.

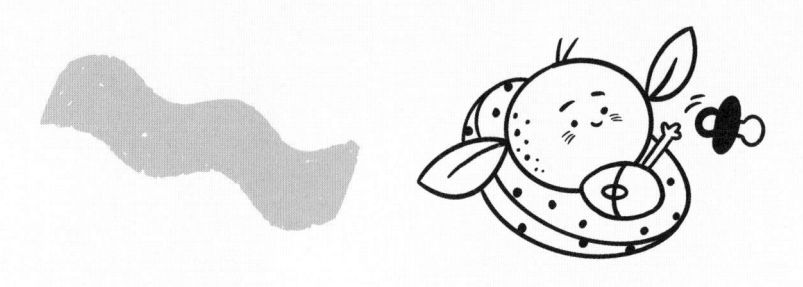

Unfortunately, some core beliefs are negative, and these can become deeply entrenched from a young age. Negative core beliefs are formed when you're repeatedly subjected to a negative experience or emotion, such as being made to feel belittled, ashamed, neglected or unloved. These beliefs are formed and reinforced in various ways, such as through repeated verbal or physical punishment, or through the threat of violence or neglect. These core beliefs might not be true – in fact, they probably aren't – but your inner goblin doesn't know enough yet to understand this. I hadn't done anything wrong that day at the school fair, but the message I received was that my intentions are often misunderstood, I wasn't good enough, that I always mess up, and it struck me deeply. When these messages are repeated and reinforced, we can't rationalize them as we're not equipped with the ability to do that as children; instead, we internalize them.

I want to be clear here that negative core beliefs are only developed through *repeated* messages. **No parent is perfect**, and there will always be times when adults respond to their children in ways that could be better. We all have our own struggles – doing your best with what you've got is what matters! Understanding how negative core beliefs are formed is important because it can help you to avoid reinforcing negative messages – and it might also help you to recognize some of the moments from your own upbringing where your own core beliefs were formed. Even when we know this, we're not going to be perfect. I'm definitely not perfect – no one is.

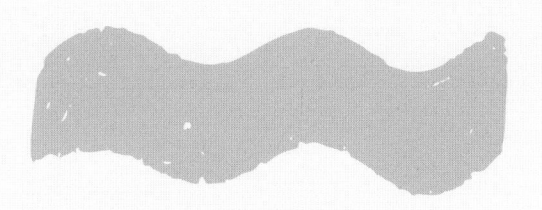

One of my own negative core beliefs is that I'm somehow misunderstood, and that people will be disappointed/dislike me when they get to know me. As an adult, I have evidence that this isn't true all of the time, but my inner child/inner goblin still feels this way, no matter how much I rationalize or tell myself that it's not the case. What makes this belief even trickier to navigate is that it often isn't *purely* an irrational thought. It is, in part, a protective adaptation, an alertness to the fact that being misunderstood has happened many times before. If you are neurodivergent, are disabled or are different to societal norms in some way, you will likely see some of this in you. There is a fine line to tread between trying to challenge the fear, but not so much that you face very real social consequences.

Core beliefs like this are painful; no one wants to feel disapproved of, misunderstood, unloved, unwanted or abandoned. And so we develop ways of interacting with the world to try to cover up or avoid these feelings. There are many different strategies we might develop as a kind of armour for these painful deep feelings.

23

One of the most common strategies is people-pleasing.

People-pleasing

Before going into this, I want to be clear that core beliefs like the ones I've described might not necessarily lead to people-pleasing as a strategy. Some people might develop other strategies, such as avoidance, not letting people in, or even doing the opposite of people-pleasing! Defence strategies are complex. But people-pleasing is a common one, and one I really struggle with personally. It's something that can get in the way of me being 'authentically me', because I'm focused entirely on other people liking me and finding me palatable, regardless of my own happiness – or whether I even like them back!

It's great and admirable and amazing to want to make everyone around you happy! But people-pleasing means taking this to an extreme, and pushing aside your own needs and boundaries in favour of other people's comfort. It's doing everything in your power to avoid conflict, to the detriment of your own happiness. It's thinking, **I need people to like me, no matter what.**

You may feel that if you please everyone around you, you won't have to deal with feeling like a disappointment. At least, that's how I often feel. You might think that if you just agree with what others say and don't cause any conflict, you can safely continue holding that familiar belief of my feelings don't matter. Even though this is a painful belief to hold, it's also comforting in its familiarity, and the thought of pushing back against it might seem insurmountable. It's like your beliefs are a frequently travelled rocky terrain, but it's familiar – there's a narrow path you've carved into it over the years of travelling through. There *could* be another easier path, but what if that road is even rockier? What if you don't have the right kind of vehicle or tools to get past some tricky obstacles? And who knows where that unknown path may lead, and if there is a way to turn back.

But ultimately, that unfamiliar path leads to somewhere you can rest – maybe a spa where you can look after yourself. Somewhere much calmer than the predictable destination of the rocky terrain you'd carved out for years and years. **There are tools and ways to take this other path**, which we will move on to later in this chapter.

These are the problems with people-pleasing.

● You lose sight of your boundaries.

Your boundaries might become undefined or even impossible for you to recognize. You might start doing things you don't enjoy in order to make other people like you. You might start to lose your sense of who you really are – your authentic yourself.

● It's an unsustainable strategy.

Constantly people-pleasing means that when you encounter someone who doesn't like you (and it is going to happen at some point), it's an unbearable feeling. Deep down, it brings you back to that vulnerable child who felt so unsafe and unsure. You never want that to happen again, so you might start thinking of ways to avoid situations where people might not like you. Maybe you'll ruminate on what you've said or done 'wrong', and think about what to do differently in the future so that people don't dislike you again (this is so me), or so you don't cause any conflict. You build up your defences further, while the core belief remains unchallenged, and possibly even strengthened.

That day at the school fair, the experience led me to try to protect myself by deciding that I would never do something like that again. In other words, **I was building up my armour with avoidance**. I also ruminated a lot on what I'd done 'wrong', even though I knew deep down that I hadn't done anything bad. I was a child, but not so young that I couldn't recognize that I was being misunderstood, that the lady who shouted was probably having her own issues or a bad day. But that was all pushed aside – it didn't matter; all that mattered was not causing conflict and avoiding being in a situation like that again.

And so you learn that in order to keep the people around you happy, you must look after their needs to the detriment of your own. You swallow your own feelings just to keep the peace. This can (but not always) lead to feelings of resentment building up, and suddenly exploding. I used to follow this pattern, and it took me a while to realize what was happening. People-pleasing can also lead to you behaving passive-aggressively rather than being assertive about your own needs and boundaries.

Core beliefs are very powerful and deeply ingrained. They aren't just something you can shake off easily. We all rationally understand that not everyone is going to like us, but at the same time it hurts more than it should when it does happen. This is an important distinction; even those who aren't people-pleasers are affected when other people don't like them – everyone is! But the difference is that when it happens, they don't feel like they have to change themselves to make everyone else around them happy. If they've done something wrong, they don't feel like they have to dwell on it for hours or days or even longer; they are able to rationally recognize their error, apologize and make amends if needed. And if they haven't done anything wrong and someone is unhappy with them simply for being them or for some subjective reason, they can process that, move on, and not ruminate on it to a detrimental degree. Sounds pretty great, right?

If you're a people-pleaser like me, the idea of being able to process things in that rational way might seem impossible – but awareness is power. Once you understand your core beliefs and the defence mechanisms you've built around them, you can start to recognize areas of your life where they're affecting you. And once you recognize them, you can start to challenge them.

This doesn't mean you can easily get rid of them! I still have my negative core beliefs, and I'm still a people-pleaser (in recovery!). Sometimes I'm more of a people-pleaser, and that tends to be during times when I have to allocate more energy to other areas of my life such as work, or trying to deal with too many conflicts at once. Like most things, **becoming a non-people-pleaser isn't something that happens that you can just tick off a list.** It takes continual intention. You might be able to pay less attention to it as time goes on, but it always needs some honing. Sometimes more rocks and rubble fall into the road along the route to the relaxing spa, and they need chucking out of the way. So I try to spot these obstacles and chip away at them bit by bit, which leads to chipping away at those limiting core beliefs.

I recently had an experience that showed me how far I've come.

> **'Awareness is power.'**

I've always struggled to motivate myself to exercise, so in recent years I've started attending group classes. That in itself is something I'm proud of, because going to these classes meant challenging my own social anxieties and overcoming my avoidance. I quickly realized that no one really cares; everyone is just there to move their bodies, and all that matters is that I'm moving mine. I enjoyed going to these classes and feeling inspired by others around me.

I'd just moved to a new area, so I decided to join a local Pilates class. I called the instructor beforehand to book in and just to confirm that it was OK for me to join, because I know my limitations – I'm not putting myself down here, I'm just being realistic. I wanted to make sure that I'd be going into a comfortable environment. He said, 'We'll look after you!' So I thought, Great. I was excited about getting back into doing a regular class.

On the day, I got dressed in a comfy baggy T-shirt and leggings, and made my way to class. At first, everything seemed fine. As the class progressed, though, I began to feel that the instructor was repeatedly drawing attention to me more than anyone in the group. He was making corrections to my form, which is of course a good thing to do, and an important part of being in a class and learning. But it was beginning to cross a subtle line and I began to start questioning what was going on. But at this stage, I told myself it was fine, he meant well, and that he probably didn't realize how he was making me feel.

Then something happened that made me feel deeply uncomfortable.

We were doing tiptoe squats, and I was moving my hands to help me keep my balance. The instructor pointed at my wiggly hands and said, 'Are we making shit up now?'

I must have looked confused, because he repeated the comment, this time adding an impression of me wiggling my fingers.

I decided he'd meant it as a joke, so although it made me feel under scrutiny and ill at ease, I tried to laugh it off. **No need to make an issue of it,** I thought.

Then he turned to one of my classmates, who I could tell was a regular. He spoke under his breath, but it was still loud enough for me to hear. He said, 'That's what you get when you piss about.'

This is how my thoughts went at that point:

He could be joking – it could just be 'banter'.

It might not even be related to me.

But...

It's not appropriate for him to talk that way when he's in a position of power. He doesn't know me or how it might make me feel.

And...

Regardless of whether it's 'just a joke' or unrelated to me, the very fact that I am having to think about this – and the fact that it's making me uncomfortable – is all that matters.

I don't have to stay in this class and quietly cover my discomfort, laugh and pretend to be chill and cool 'because it's just banter'.

I can just leave.

The old me would've said nothing, stayed until the end of the class, and then just not gone back – better to eat your own discomfort than say how you feel or honour your boundaries, because that causes CONFLICT and people DEFINITELY not liking you, and there's nothing worse than that.

But I wanted to challenge myself, and I figured this was a good situation in which to do so, because I had nothing to lose.

So I asked him, 'What did you just say?'

He said, 'Nothing.'

Whenever I get angry or frustrated, I get shaky and tearful. And so I stood there for a long second, feeling frozen and angry, unable to say much because otherwise I'd start to rage-cry (you will know this feeing if you're the same!).

But as I stood there, I realized that what had happened was one of two things. Either he had actively wanted to make me feel uncomfortable, and had done so under the guise of 'banter' – or he hadn't meant to do it, but he'd still acted inappropriately and, in his position as an instructor, he should have known better. Either way, it wasn't a situation I was enjoying. Whether he meant to or not, he'd crossed my boundaries.

So I walked out.

And as I walked away and let the rage-tears fall, I felt SO proud of myself.

I was crying for all the times in the past where I had stayed in the bad situation despite it making me feel terrible.

I was crying because there was still that inner voice telling me, 'They're going to think you're boring and oversensitive, and that you're crying just because of a bit of harmless banter.'

Note
this really links to the 'Vulnerability' chapter

And I was crying because I DID IT. I stuck to my boundaries.

It doesn't matter what anyone else thought of me in that class. I had respected myself.

I shared this story on my social media because I was proud. The instructor called me afterwards, but it was not to make a genuine apology or to check if I was OK. He said, 'I'm sorry that you feel that way.' He said, 'I was just making a joke.' He said, 'Everyone was shocked that you walked out like that. No one else has a problem with me.' He was making excuses and trying to blame me for the way I had felt.

Again, the old me probably would have accepted that. It's easier to do that than to be the one causing conflict, the one pushing back. But I told him assertively and politely that even if he'd meant no harm, he should acknowledge that that kind of banter isn't professional or appropriate. He refused to accept this, but it didn't matter – because I had stuck up for myself!

'Indirect microaggressions and unkind "banter" can be hard to call out, especially in situations where there's an imbalance of power.'

When I shared this story on my social media, a lot of people messaged me to say they'd had similar experiences in gyms and exercise classes. It's such a shame because it puts people off going (although there are of course lots of great gyms and classes that do create a genuinely safe space for their clients).

Indirect microaggressions and unkind 'banter' can be hard to call out, especially in situations where there's an imbalance of power. If you take a stand and call out a bully, you might be accused of being oversensitive – which is why it's sometimes easier to pretend to be tough when it happens, and act like it doesn't bother you. The instructor's behaviour that day made me feel uncomfortable, but he wasn't being openly horrible or aggressive in a way where everyone present would automatically agree that he was in the wrong. I had to be assertive and express my discomfort, while taking the risk that the instructor and the other people in the class might feel I was making a big deal over nothing.

In some ways, this was a relatively straightforward opportunity for me to overcome my people-pleasing instinct and stand up for myself. It was a gym class, and that meant I had the freedom to walk away and to decide not to come back. It can be more complex if the situation takes place in your workplace or during an interaction with a friend, partner or family member – you can't always walk away from things, and if you know you've got to go back to work the next day or that you want to continue to have this person in your life, sometimes it can feel easier to just shrug it off or tell yourself you aren't really that upset. Resolving these situations in a way that honours your boundaries can be complicated and challenging, without a simple answer – but as hard as it can be to step away from people-pleasing, it can also be very liberating.

Recovery from people-pleasing

Being a people-pleaser in recovery isn't easy – and it isn't straightforward. It can sometimes leave you open to conflict and criticism.

It's important to note that being a people-pleaser in recovery doesn't mean being rude or unkind to other people! It's not about choosing to start arguments or trying to push others around. It's just about being the best version of you, and respecting yourself and your boundaries. Recovering from people-pleasing helps you to be authentically you, and it also helps the people around you to understand you and like you – *for you*. You can't please everyone, and if you try, it will only lead to stress and resentment, which can build up over time until they become unmanageable. It's much better to assertively communicate your boundaries and hold people accountable as you go along.

What can I do to recover from people-pleasing?

If you think you are a people-pleaser and you want to try to break the habit (and it's OK if now is not the time for you), it could be helpful to ask yourself the following questions:
- What are my core beliefs?
- Why do I have these core beliefs?
- What are my boundaries?
- What am I doing that's people-pleasing?
- Why do I want to stop people-pleasing? (My answer to this one was: **'So that I can be true to me!'**)

Challenge your assumptions
Ask yourself whether you have any assumptions about what people will think of you if you say 'no' or assert your boundaries. Is your brain trying to trick you (brains are notoriously good at this), and telling you that standing up for yourself will make others upset and angry? Try to think of some occasions when you've observed other people saying 'no' or asserting their boundaries, and nothing bad has happened. Perhaps you can remember a time when a friend asserted a boundary with you, and you weren't upset or offended by them doing so.

Challenging your people-pleasing behaviour
Try to identify some situations in which you can begin to challenge your people-pleasing behaviour. As mentioned earlier, some situations are more complicated than others. If you've been friends with someone for years and they're used to your people-pleasing ways, they may be alarmed or upset if you suddenly start asserting yourself strongly. It's not likely to go down well if you suddenly say 'I've pretended _____ has been OK for five years and now I'm telling you it's never been OK!!!' and they have no clue why you haven't mentioned this before. Situations with coworkers can also be especially hard because you probably need the money and the job. At first, look for some easier (and small) ways to challenge your people-pleasing, until you feel more confident with it. Practise saying 'no' to smaller, less important things. This point is continued in the 'Recovery isn't a straight line' section on page 41.

The power of 'no'
You've probably heard the saying: '"No" is a complete sentence.' And it is. It's OK to simply tell someone you don't want to do something. Or you might feel more comfortable sharing a reason, and that's OK too.

The more you say 'no', the easier it will become. **Remember, assertiveness is completely different to aggression.** Being assertive is just advocating for how you feel, while also valuing and considering the other person. Practise being assertive when you say 'no', or when you have an issue to raise or need to set a boundary.

Every time you say 'no' to something you don't want to do or that makes you uncomfortable, you are healing your inner goblin. You are advocating for yourself, and getting closer to your authentic you.

There will be challenges, of course, because those core beliefs and defences are strong. They've had years to build up layers of armour, after all. When I come across these challenges, I try to tell myself the following:
- You can care for people while also not being responsible for how everyone else feels.
- You can say 'no' and still be a nice person.
- You can disagree with a friend and still be loved.
- You can walk away from a situation and still be an accepting person.
- You can set a boundary and still be a kind person.

These may be helpful for you too! Or you can come up with your own reminders.

There's a saying I like: **'What you don't do determines what you can do.'** In other words, saying 'yes' to everyone means you may run out of energy and find you are ultimately unable to say 'yes' to the things that really matter to you. I have learned that it's important for me to set boundaries so that I am able to do the things I need to do and to be there for the people I care about. This is especially true since becoming more ill with chronic migraine recently, and I really had to think about how I was spending my valuable time. We each have our own finite tank, and we can't run on empty.

If a random person dislikes you after you set boundaries and respect yourself in a kind and assertive way, they are not people who truly care for you. If it's an important person in your life doing this, you could have a positive discussion with them about it and turn things around. It's not the be-all and end-all: we all make mistakes and cross boundaries, sometimes without realizing it.

Being realistic
I want to stress that **being a people pleaser isn't a character flaw.** As I mentioned previously, some of these defences are likely very real protective adaptations that you've built up over time. They build up from repeated instances where you have tried to respect your boundaries, and were rejected for doing so.

Learning to say no is not simply about saying the right words. It's important to first address your past experiences and the social reality of which you live in, which will be different for me and for you. Not everyone faces the same social consequences for saying no.

There have been many times when I've said 'no' and it hasn't gone down well. It's been met with anger or disappointment. Sometimes it's resolved itself in time, sometimes it just hasn't.

What you **DON'T** do determines what you **CAN** do.

This is why it's got to be a gradual practice, little 'no's slipped in here and there where possible. And try not compare yourself to someone else who you may see as more assertive. They may be in a position where there aren't as many social consequences to them saying no.

Recovery isn't a straight line
It's totally normal to feel like you're reverting to people-pleasing sometimes – I often do it. The important thing is to reflect on it, so you can understand what you're doing and why. Sometimes you might find you just don't have the emotional energy to tackle the situation – and sometimes it's just not worth it (especially with family situations or workplace disagreements). Realistically, there are bound to be certain situations where you don't have the social capital or power to challenge what's happening, and where simply walking away is not an option. If you find yourself reverting to people-pleasing behaviours in scenarios like this, it doesn't mean you've 'failed'; it just means that life and relationships are complicated. It's OK to pick your battles, as long as you stay aware of your boundaries and who you are – never lose sight of that. And keep practising saying 'no' and respecting yourself when you can.

People-pleasing as a defence strategy can become really ingrained. I'm still fighting it myself, and sometimes I lose (but sometimes I win!). Sometimes I have to be strategic. Sometimes there are other more pressing things that take over my mind. **But what matters is the trajectory.** Recovery isn't a straight line, but if I look back to the way I was ten years ago, I can say I am much improved now. So I know it's hard to do in practice, but remind yourself of the slow, slow progress!

2

Finding the people and spaces that bring you calm and joy

When we're young (and also when we're old!), we all do stuff that makes no sense to us. I'm going to share my example of something I did at the age of 21 that I look back on and could never imagine doing now. I still can't quite believe I thought it was a good idea at the time.

I explained this briefly in the main introduction, and I'll go into a lot more detail in chapter four, but I grew up with severe social anxiety and dealt with selective mutism throughout my time at school. Things improved when I was at university, but these were still challenges for me.

And what did I decide to do when university finished?

I moved into a shared house: five strangers, plus me.

When I had gone to university a few years before, I had lived with other people, and some of them had gone on to become my closest friends. So now that university was over, I thought I'd just... do it again.

Then I would have MORE friends!

I didn't consider the fact that I had nothing in common with anyone living there. I didn't even think about the fact that I might feel uncomfortable. To be honest, I didn't think it really mattered how I felt; it just mattered that other people liked me (a clear example of how extreme people-pleasing leads to losing your sense of who you are).

I signed a one-year contract and moved in – and quickly realized I'd made a mistake. My issues with social anxiety and selective mutism came roaring back. I spent the whole year never going into the shared kitchen or living area (I would only buy foods that didn't require cooking or other prep), tiptoeing past my housemates' bedrooms on the way to my top-floor bedroom while thinking, **Please no one see me, please no one see me**, over and over, and not daring to make any audible sound in my room in case I inadvertently reminded the others that I existed.

I ended up taking on as many extra hours as possible at work, and spending most nights staying at my friend EJ's house.

My housemates were perfectly nice people. They just weren't my people. And the space wasn't the space where I could be me.

I'm sure you can think of examples of times when you've made choices or taken actions that didn't help you to thrive. There are a lot of reasons why this can happen. Sometimes, especially when it comes to things such as housing or work situations, you may be in a situation where **there is literally no other choice**. There are real-world restrictions that affect your ability to choose your preferred people and space. Perhaps you can't afford to live alone, or have care needs (or caring responsibilities) that mean you have to make certain decisions. That was certainly part of it for me; the house-share was my cheapest option. But also, part of what contributes to these decisions is that we don't know ourselves well enough, and that was true for me. I didn't know what I needed.

Finding out what you need

My chaotic upbringing meant that I'd never really had that sense of 'home'. When you don't have a sense of what 'home' is, you don't naturally look for it, because you don't know that it exists. In fact, you might even make choices that actively lead you away from the things that would bring you a sense of comfort and safety, and towards the things that will bring you discomfort and chaos, because that's all you know.

> **'When you don't have a sense of what 'home' is, you don't naturally look for it, because you don't know that it exists.'**

We can struggle to have insight into what we need for many overlapping reasons, including mental health issues, physical health issues, past traumas, neurodivergence and many more.

If you have grown up or lived in an environment in which your basic needs were not met, you might not have a real understanding of what those basic needs are. I felt as though I knew what they were on a logical level, but I didn't *truly* know them. They aren't solid. They're hidden behind a translucent curtain.

You might have heard of Maslow's hierarchy of needs. Abraham Maslow was a psychologist, and his hierarchy of needs is usually presented as a triangle or pyramid. I'm going to show it as a five-tiered cake though, because it's just more fun. The base sponge represents our physiological needs: things like food (cake! Though that's not so nutritious), shelter and warmth. The next sponge is our safety needs; when these needs are met, we feel sure that we're not in danger, and that we're not going to find ourselves in a situation in the near future where our physiological needs are unmet. Sponge number three is our social needs: a sense of belonging and a feeling that we are with people we love and can trust. The next tasty sponge is our self-esteem, which will vary from person to person, but is closely tied to our core beliefs, which we mentioned in the previous chapter. The most delicious sponge layer, self-actualization, is about feeling that we are being deeply and authentically ourselves.

Because it's a pyramid, it's hard to build up to the higher parts without a secure base made up of the lower parts. They aren't less important; they're the essential foundations. It's important to mention this to be realistic, rather than negative: there's no point in being hard on yourself for not being fortunate enough to have the base layers. There are so many factors that are out of our control that affect this. There are ways to progress too – it just isn't as straightforward as just 'pull yourself up by your bootstraps'.

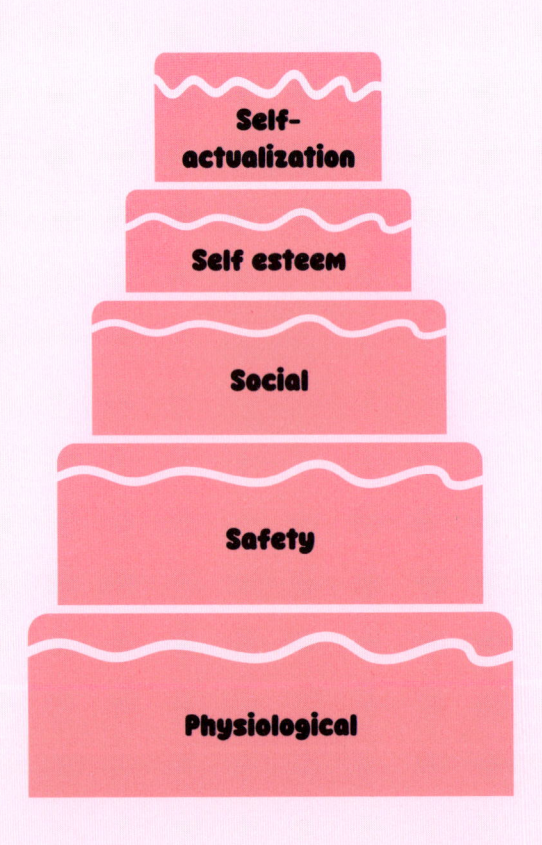

- Self-actualization
- Self esteem
- Social
- Safety
- Physiological

So for me, the first two base cake layers are built, which I am grateful for, and the social layer is almost there but a bit crumbly (it fluctuates) – because if, like me, you grew up in an environment in which you didn't feel safe or secure, it might be harder for you to recognize what you need in order to achieve that feeling of safety, and then to build on that to the next stage of the pyramid. And then the self-esteem cake layer above is halfway there – it's not the best foundation for the top layer, but there must be a little bit of self-actualization wobbling on top, otherwise I wouldn't be writing this book!

Here are some questions I find helpful to ask myself – and that hopefully could be helpful for you, to really straightforwardly ask yourself about your needs and what they look like. Try to think of a time in the past where you've made a decision or found yourself in a situation that hasn't been right for you. It's important to note that this is not about regret or berating yourself for doing the wrong thing; **these challenges give us an opportunity to learn**, and as much as I hated living in that house, it taught me a valuable lesson about myself. Ideally, the past is for reflection, not rumination – though rumination does still happen, and I do do it from time to time.

'The past is for reflection, not rumination.'

- Why do you think you made this decision? Could it have been because of people-pleasing tendencies? Did you have a specific goal in mind (like my plan to make friends) that then didn't materialize? Were you being impulsive and making a snap decision in the moment?

- What past experiences might have led you to make this choice?

- How soon did you realize it wasn't the right choice for you? What were the first warning signs that made you think, *I've made a mistake*?

- Based on your answers to the above, are there any questions you can ask yourself in future when faced with similar decisions?

It's OK if you don't know how to answer all these questions. I do not know all the answers all of the time, I just know what to ask myself. Getting to know ourselves takes time: it's ongoing and not always easy. Sit with the questions and reflect on what happened, to see if you can come away with a firmer sense of what you might need in future. It's also important to remember that your needs are going to constantly change throughout your life – and so will other people's.

This might all seem like a bit of a negative start, but don't worry – it's not all chores and questions, this is the fun chapter! If the last chapter was about saying 'no', this chapter is about getting to say 'yes'. It's about finding your people and creating your own space. It's not about analyzing the negative, but about curiosity and inviting people in.

I was lost for a long time, with people-pleasing issues, social anxiety, and suspected autism and trauma. There was a lot of noise going on, and that made it hard to know what I wanted for myself. And though I'm doing a LOT better now, **I'm still figuring things out**. I'm still learning about myself, and I still feel confused about what I'm doing a lot of the time.

These days, I feel lucky to have a sense of 'home'. For me, this is not just the space where I live, but also my partner Nabil, my friends and my cats. Nabil cannot fathom why I ever did things like moving into that house, by the way. It's bizarre to him why anyone would ever do something that clearly isn't going to suit them, because he has a much firmer sense of what he needs. I love that, because I learn so much from him.

Be more cat

Whether you're feeling quite lost, like I was in my early twenties, or you have a good idea of what you want and need, like Nabil, we all have our own circumstances and difficulties to handle. There's no one answer fits all when it comes to finding the right people and spaces for you. But I do think we can all probably learn a little something on this front from my cats, Inki and Mochi (and cats in general, really).

Inki and Mochi don't even have to think about these things; they just *know*. If someone doesn't feel right to them or crosses their boundaries, they're not going to hang about. They might accept food from someone they're not keen on, just because they want to eat, but they're not going to be choosing that person's lap to sit on. They're not going to settle for sleeping where I want them to, either; they will sleep in the comfiest cardboard box I've discarded and ignore their cat beds. They think about their *own* comfort and look after their *own* needs. Of course, cats and other pets with loving owners are fortunate in that they don't have to work and they have a safe home, a personal chef and all the time they like to chill, whereas we humans typically have a lot more to deal with. But we can keep that little inner cat part of us as a reminder of what our boundaries would be if we *didn't* have to deal with all the things that humans have to deal with!

Finding your people

This is a tricky topic, because however much we might want to, we can't control or impact what others do. Just like I couldn't automatically make five new best friends just by moving into a house; we can't just decide 'I want to meet a new friend' or 'I want to get a partner'. That's not how things work. So when it comes to finding your people, it's not just a case of seeking them out (although that is part of it), it's also about recognizing them: **understanding who the right people are in the first place**.

What changed things for me was a combination of trying to work on my people-pleasing, and a whole bunch of luck. As I tackled my people-pleasing tendencies, I started to see that the right people for me were the ones who would love me along with my boundaries, my weaknesses and strengths.

Finding the right people for you is never black and white. Sometimes you just don't know what (or who!) you want, and that's normal. You will probably find you want some people in certain spaces and not others – for example, you might have a colleague you love working with, but you wouldn't want to go on holiday with them or live with them.

I have always loved board games, and so it occurred to me that joining a local board game club might be a more effective way of meeting people with whom I had things in common than moving into a house full of strangers and hoping for the best. So I went along to a local board game evening – and I ended up meeting Nabil.

I want to be clear that I didn't go there looking for anyone in particular, like a partner! I went alone, and when I arrived, he was in charge of the entry fees. He told me how much it was, and I ducked down to root through my bag and find my purse. I've always done this; it might not be the most elegant approach, but when I need to get something out of my bag, I squat down and rummage away.

From Nabil's perspective, though, the person he was talking to had just ducked down underneath the table and disappeared. I looked up to see him peering over the desk and down at me with an amused expression on his face.

We didn't become a couple right away; we were friends for a while first. Nabil owns the board game company that runs these events, though I didn't realize it at the time. Once, when he told me I didn't have to pay, I asked him, 'But won't you get in trouble?'

So I might not have realized it right away, that day when I was ducking down behind the desk to dig through my bag – but I was one step closer to 'home'.

one step closer to HOME

Of course, I am not saying that all you need to do to find your own version of Nabil is go along to a local board game club – as I've said before, so much of this is down to good luck. But I wanted to share this story to highlight the big difference in how I felt in each situation. In the shared house, even though my housemates were perfectly nice people, I felt uncomfortable, on edge and out of place. I lived there, but I didn't belong there. But for whatever reason, from the moment I stepped into the board game event that evening, I felt comfortable and at ease; I wasn't too shy to chat to Nabil, or afraid to be myself and squat down to root through my bag. It was a space and a group of people to which I felt I could belong.

Friendships change – and that's OK

As we age and grow, and our lives change, we evolve as people – and that can mean our friendships evolve too. Sometimes, it means they get better – you might get closer, like Nabil and I did – but sometimes it can mean letting go of a friendship that no longer makes you happy, or just accepting that it's not the same as it used to be. As you get to know yourself better, you might realize that what you thought was a fun and healthy friendship is actually a bit one-sided or even toxic, or it could just be that you and that person are no longer at the same places in your lives, and that all of your wants and needs no longer align, but you're still friends.

When we notice a shift like this in a friendship that we don't want to let go of, it can be hard to know what to do. Nobody is perfect, and you might know that ultimately, this is someone you love and care about, and you want to be in your life, but there is a certain aspect of the friendship that makes you feel uncomfortable. Perhaps you have a friend who is prone to gossip. Gossip is one of those guilty pleasures that, like most people, I participate in (the nice kind of gossip, I like to think)! But it can also leave me feeling a bit yuck afterwards – for example, I have a friend who gossips a lot and, logically, I find myself wondering what they say about me when I'm not around.

There are different ways that different people might deal with this. Some might openly say, 'I don't want to gossip any more,' although that feels a bit too confrontational for me – I'm not quite there yet, but if you are, you should be proud! My strategy is to try to change the topic when things get a bit too gossipy. You might also decide to set a boundary for yourself by not sharing things with this person, unless you don't care about other people finding out.

I find that as I work on getting to know myself better, I recognize the people who drain me, and the people who lift me up – and **I can reflect on what I don't want in my life, and also what I do want**.

As you learn to recognize what true friendship looks like for you, you'll have a much clearer idea of who you want around you.

Ask yourself:

- Who makes you feel safe and calm?

- What is it about them that makes you feel that way?

- Who do you feel most yourself around?

- If you have people in your life who don't make you feel safe/calm/yourself, why are they in your life? Is there something about them that you really value, or is this your people-pleasing tendencies at play?

- If it's the former, is there anything you can do to set a personal boundary or manage the friendship so that it feels a bit safer for you?

- If it's the latter, what do you think is happening in the friendship?

This is not an instruction to cut off anyone who doesn't completely align with you! It's an exercise in understanding *why* different people are in your life. We are complicated, multilayered creatures (to our benefit and to our detriment), and often there isn't a clear answer, but reflecting on these questions will hopefully help you get to know yourself a little better.

You are one of your people
I want to end this section on 'Finding your people' by reminding you that **you are one of them**. You're the person you spend the most time with, after all. So although it can be hard to meet people, and it's not possible to just wave a magic wand and have friends, you can pay attention to being a good friend to yourself. This isn't just in the way you speak to yourself and treat yourself, but also in the way you spend time with yourself. It's easy to assume that certain activities are just for couples or friendship groups, but it's not always the case. You can go to the cinema alone; you can go out for coffee or for dinner alone; you can go to a concert or a play or an art gallery alone. Of course, there are some things for which you do need other people – like playing (most) board games or taking part in team sports – but this can be a great opportunity to join a club or a team and perhaps meet some fun people. It's also OK to just not want friends in the same way other people do.

Finding your space

I find so much joy in creating an environment that makes me feel calm and happy, so I had to include a section on this. It's not just about *who* you want around you, but *what* you want to be surrounded with. This might sound materialistic, but it doesn't have to be about objects and buying things. It can be about arranging your space in a way that soothes you, and finding small ways to make sure your living space feels cozy and works for you.

You don't always have to have everything in place to begin making changes. You may not be in a position to move into your own home. You may be renting, and therefore unable to paint the walls or hang pictures. **That doesn't mean you have to delay joy**: you can bring it in in small ways. Little things – such as bedsheets, a lamp, a candle or a cushion – can change your space.

Everyone has their own ideal home environment. Some people feel soothed by clean, minimalist lines; others want to fill their homes with things that they love, so wherever they look, they'll see something that brings them joy. I really struggle with bright lights, as they aggravate my chronic migraine and make me feel overwhelmed, so for me, a comforting home space is one with low lighting, perhaps a few lamps dotted around. The overhead light – the dreaded 'big light' – never gets turned on in my home! Here are a few of the things in my home that bring me little pops of joy whenever I see them:

- My plants

- Bright colours – from a full wall-sized mural to little accessories scattered around

- Shelves filled with my favourite books and games

- Soft, comfortable blankets on sofas and chairs, ready to be snuggled under

- A pink Christmas tree (which I keep up all the time and decorate for different occasions, such as Chinese New Year or Halloween)

- Pretty lamps

- Candles

- My collection of plushies

Your own aesthetic and comfort needs will be different. Look around your home now. What are the items that delight you? Is there anything you can see that makes you feel unhappy or uneasy? Why is it there? Of course, some things are necessities, even if we don't always like the way they look – such as medical equipment, appliances or radiators – but if you're finding yourself looking at something you don't need – perhaps a stack of old books you've been meaning to take to the charity shop, or a pile of laundry that needs sorting – ask yourself whether you are in a position to do yourself the kindness of changing it. Of course, these things take energy and effort, and you might not be able to deal with them all the time, but **looking after your space is an act of kindness to yourself**, and can help you to feel soothed and recharged.

It's all about calming your nervous system. We typically can't control everything in our lives – you might have a stressful job or a challenging commute, or be battling health issues – but if you can try to create a soothing environment in your home, even if it's just in one corner, it can make a big difference. So ask yourself:

- What brings you joy?

- What do you need around you so that you function best?

- What is holding you back from making these changes?

Your home environment can also serve as an early warning system for when things are starting to overwhelm you. Again, this will be different for everyone, but I know that when my home is starting to feel cluttered or messy, with dishes or laundry piling up, it can often be a sign that I'm getting overwhelmed in other ways, and it flags to me that I need to start looking after myself with more care.

As you probably know, I love baking, and I think it can serve as a useful analogy for the things we've discussed in this chapter. Finding the spaces and people that bring you joy can be a bit like baking a cake. There are some key ingredients that you need to create a cake, no matter what kind – these are like the base of the pyramid shown on page 48. Once you have that foundation in place, you can start to consider the other ingredients that will work for you, and perhaps even the ways in which you want to adorn your cake with icing or other decorations. **Remember, it's your cake**; you're not baking it for someone else. We all have different needs, and we all flourish under different conditions.

So – what do you want in your cake?

3

'Fake it till you make it' and imposter phenomenon

When I was around 24, I was working as a psychological wellbeing practitioner within the NHS. My role involved working with people for short one-to-one sessions, usually about 20 to 30 minutes each, during which I'd support them in using CBT strategies to help manage their anxiety and depression. It was a stressful job, but a rewarding one too.

The issue at the time was, I didn't 'feel' like a therapist. I had all the tools; I'd studied the techniques and I knew how to share them effectively. But I noticed that I had this idea in my head of what a therapist looked and sounded like – and I didn't match up with that idea.

So I started to try to make changes. As I will discuss further in chapter eight, I love colourful clothing and cute accessories, but the idea of a therapist I held in my head was someone who wore dark, serious clothing in muted colours. So that's what I wore. I also spoke more like I thought a therapist should, and even changed the way I sat, making sure I was sitting bolt upright with my feet on the floor, when my natural tendency is to sit cross-legged or sort of bundled up.

Was this a case of 'fake it till you make it'? Was I just trying to look the part? Or was I trying to change things about myself because I was worried that who I really was just wasn't good enough?

I am a Good Therapist

I am a bad therapist

Fake it till you make it

Looking back, I think I would probably have been a happier and possibly better therapist if I had shown up more as myself; if I had worn clothes that more accurately expressed who I was, and if I'd had a bit more faith in my ability to help people as me, rather than hiding my personality away. I didn't feel like a therapist; instead, I felt like I was projecting an image of a 'good therapist'.

I suppose my idea of professionalism was quite narrow. I used a particular voice, a sort of 'customer service' voice, and tried to follow certain conventions that I wouldn't usually adhere to. For example, I felt like I had to start every session with a bit of small talk – 'How was your week? Was your drive here OK?' – when small talk isn't something I particularly enjoy, and I suspect many of the patients I was speaking to didn't enjoy it either (especially when you consider how short our sessions were in the first place).

Of course, it's not entirely straightforward. There are always certain rules or conventions that we do have to abide by in certain situations – for example, in my role as a therapist, I needed to stick to the techniques we'd been taught to use, such as active listening, and there would always be certain things it would be inappropriate for me to say or do. These are important to practise, but there is a distinction between professionalism and changing things about myself so I would seem like the idealised version of a therapist I had in my mind. Parts of my personality that, perhaps, could actually have enabled me to build a more honest connection with the patients I was speaking to. The therapeutic relationship is the most important thing, and it is possible to show up as yourself in a way that is an act of care towards the patient. It also makes the therapeutic relationship easier to judge from the start, because you're both being yourselves.

Reflection point

- **Have you ever faked it till you made it?**

- **And if you 'made it', what did that look like for you?**

- **Would you do things differently now?**

We've all heard the advice 'Fake it till you make it.' It can be well meaning, and for a long time, it was my entire mantra for life. I won't totally lambast the idea, because it worked for me in certain instances. (There is even research to suggest that putting on a fake smile can make you feel more positive – although this research is pretty minimal, and when I tried it for myself, I just got jaw ache!). But the issue is – at what point does the faking stop? Do you ever 'make' it? The issue for me became that I felt more of an imposter, because I was always faking.

Of course, **it's not as easy as simply stopping faking it and 'just' being you** – it can be hard, and often there are reasons why we're adopting certain behaviours that might not be authentically ours.

Looking back, I want to just tell myself to bin that image of how I thought I 'should' look; to trust in my own skills and let that be the focus. But at the same time, it's not that simple. It's easy to look back at the past and criticize yourself for the way you handled things, but it's important to give yourself grace. Although I might do things differently now, I understand why I made the decisions I did then. At that time, I wasn't in the place to feel more confident in myself, and that's OK. It needed to happen. And it all came down to the fact that I truly cared about the job and my patients, and I wanted to do my best.

Imposter phenomenon

For me, this idea of 'faking it till I made it' became entangled in imposter phenomenon. I was trying to fit the mould of how I thought a therapist should look and talk. But that wasn't me; the real me loves colour and doesn't 'do' small talk. As a result, I felt like a fraud wearing a therapist's costume.

Feelings of inadequacy, insecurity and feeling like a fraud happen to everyone to varying degrees; to some extent, feeling this way is completely normal. If you're a little worried about getting things right, or care so much about something that you want to make sure you do as well as possible, **that is a sign that you're passionate about what you're doing**. Where this moves from caring a great deal into the realm of imposter phenomenon is when you're at the upper limit; when it becomes extreme and pervasive. Imposter phenomenon is when, despite having all the skills and competence you need, you feel very strongly that you are a 'fraud', inauthentic – an imposter. It's not to be used as a way to medicalize or frame normal worries as something to be fixed.

◀ **Normal Worries**   **Imposter Phenomenon** ▶

My main skill nowadays is baking and coming up with cute baked designs, and while on some days that comes with a normal dose of self-doubt, on other days I do find myself at the imposter phenomenon end of things. It depends on my mood and my health and what I've eaten, and all the very fun background stuff like low self-esteem.

It's OK (and can be empowering) to acknowledge that you are dealing with imposter phenomenon or any kind of insecurity. **It's not weakness to admit it to yourself**. It doesn't have to define you. You can acknowledge it's there and challenge it when possible.

I want to note here that a lot of this ties into masking, a learned coping strategy many autistic people experience that involves suppressing autistic traits and trying to imitate neurotypical behaviours. Masking could be things like learning social scripts, hiding stimming or trying to mimic facial expressions. My suspected autism is probably a big explanation for my feelings of being an imposter of a therapist. Mental health professionals in particular are held to very neurotypical expectations.

I remember a comment I got on social media after being on *Bake Off*. It read: 'Mental health specialist? Looks more like the mental patient'. In other words, ***That's not how I expect a mental health professional to look and behave.*** Some of imposter phenomenon is grounded in very real societal expectations. Being different doesn't make me a bad therapist – it is simply that it doesn't fit with how many people expect me look and act. And I felt that very much to my core.

Imposter phenomenon often goes hand in hand with perfectionism, low self-esteem, people-pleasing and negative core beliefs. I definitely feel like I was dealing with imposter phenomenon when I started out as a therapist.

Identifying the cause

If you're dealing with imposter phenomenon, it can be helpful to try to identify the cause. It's key to remember that society tends to trick you into thinking that all of this is down to you as an individual, when in reality, societal factors are at play – as they so often are. Gender, age, disability and class can all affect our feelings of being an imposter. For example, women of colour are more likely to experience imposter phenomenon when working in industries with a predominantly white male workforce, due to workplace microaggressions, not receiving as much appreciation and recognition, and the overall difference in how they and their colleagues are treated. One of my best friends EJ is a very accomplished doctor, and patients often assume she is a nurse... simply because she is a woman. Then they assume the male nurse is the doctor. **Oppression and discrimination play a significant role in imposter phenomenon so cannot be ignored or dismissed**. This exists alongside difficult life experiences and the issues identified earlier, such as low self-esteem and perfectionism.

My own experiences of imposter phenomenon can be linked to a combination of factors: previous low self-esteem from my childhood experiences, and uncertainty with what I was doing. I loved working in mental health, but I didn't 100 per cent fit in with the workplace and the way it was run. We had large caseloads, barely any time with patients, and had to devote significant parts of each session to filling out quantitative questionnaires. That said, it was also very rewarding and I loved meeting everyone I did, helping with their issues and identifying their strengths.

There's a reason why imposter phenomenon only shows up in roles where there are significant demands on you (such as the workplace, being in a caring role, or taking on a position of responsibility). Learning new skills for a hobby doesn't involve the same sort of pressure, as you are less likely to be faced with the expectations of others and rules that don't suit you. For instance, I recently decided to learn to tile, and made tiling my kitchen floor my first project. Although it would've been a disaster if my tiling went wrong, at least it would be my disaster. As it turns out, I'm pretty good at tiling – even our builders commented on it. But I enjoyed the process not just because I found I was good at it, but also because I knew it wouldn't really matter if I wasn't. (Though maybe it would matter a bit, if the tiles lifted off.)

Acknowledging your imposter phenomenon, identifying what drives it and acknowledging the factors that are out of your control are building blocks towards being authentically you. It sounds like a contradiction, but **you can feel like an imposter and still be authentic with yourself** and experience joy and satisfaction from what you do. You may feel like an imposter, but you are not the phenomenon – you're you.

Ways to challenge imposter syndrome

For me, the most powerful way to challenge imposter syndrome is to recognize it for what it is. This is the theme throughout this book: knowledge is power, and self-knowledge is *more* power. If you are able to recognize imposter syndrome in yourself, that's half the battle. It's especially important to recognize the societal factors and systemic inequalities that probably can't be changed, so you can stop beating yourself up about them. You're doing everything you can.

Questions to consider

- Do you have an image of how you should look or behave in order to be accepted in a certain role? For example, do you think you need to seem 'posh' or more confident?

- Are you comparing yourself with others? (Remember that they may have more strengths in some areas, but you may have strengths they don't have. Also, you never know what's going on in other people's lives.)

- Have you been 'faking it' to make it?

- Are there any particular pressures or expectations that seem to bring out imposter phenomenon for you?

- Are you enjoying the role in which you sometimes feel imposter phenomenon? Does it let you flourish?

- Are there systematic inequalities in your workplace (or wherever you're experiencing imposter phenomenon) that might be contributing to you feeling this way?

- Do you experience any workplace microaggressions or discrimination that contribute to how you're feeling?

- What messages from childhood and society are contributing to your imposter phenomenon? (Perfectionism can play a significant role here. See if you have any thoughts like, **I haven't reached the highest level, so I must be a fraud.**)

- Do you questions your worthiness to be doing what you're doing?

- If this was a hobby, would you feel the same way?

Figuring out the answers to some of these questions (I often find a loved one or an outsider perspective helpful!) is essential to building your assuredness in your role. Remember that it's normal to still have some anxiety and worry, as long as it's not debilitating. And you probably don't ever want to be completely assured – otherwise you may be falling under the Dunning-Kruger effect...

The Dunning–Kruger effect

You'd probably heard of imposter phenomenon before, and you might also be familiar with the Dunning–Kruger effect (identified by researchers David Dunning and Justin Kruger), which is essentially the idea that people with limited knowledge or experience in certain areas tend to overestimate their abilities. In a sense, it's like the opposite of the imposter phenomenon. It's possible that some of the people you encounter in your workplace (or wherever you're experiencing imposter phenomenon) who seem to be so much more capable and confident than you are, are in fact experiencing the Dunning–Kruger effect. Confidence doesn't equal competence.

Interestingly, the researchers found that although the Dunning–Kruger effect means people start out feeling overconfident in their abilities, the more they learn about the area they were initially confident in, the more they begin to understand that they don't actually know much, and their confidence falls. Later, as they begin to learn more, their confidence grows again, but it doesn't tend to go back to that initial peak.

I have to admit, as I'm sitting here writing about the Dunning–Kruger effect, I can't help but reflect on the idea that perhaps I'm not that good at tiling after all! But perhaps that doesn't matter. If you're happy and content already, why think about it further? There's nothing wrong with it. Even if I don't have a career in tiling ahead of me, I'm still really happy with how my kitchen turned out. (Though I still think I'm pretty good at tiling.)

Another way of combating imposter phenomenon I find helpful is to practise positive affirmations that can hype yourself up. Some I like (but yours might be different – find what works for you) are:

- I've worked hard to be here, and I deserve to be here.

- Everyone is learning, all the time.
  There's no such thing as 'done'.

- Other people can do this, but nobody else can do it quite like me.

- Everyone on my team has different skills, and that's why it works.

- I'm only doubting myself because I'm NOT falling for the Dunning-Kruger effect!

- As is the case in all of these chapters, I also find it helpful to think about how other people may be thinking. Chapter nine goes into this further and I find it particularly ties in with this section.

With time and self-knowledge, you will find **realistic ways in which to show up as yourself**, whether that means talking in your 'real' voice, wearing clothes that fill you with joy, or simply approaching a situation in a way that feels more natural to you. It will be different for you than it is for me. And perhaps you'll find that you don't need to 'fake it' at all.

This is my real voice

My clothes bring me joy

Doing things differently doesn't mean doing them 'wrong'

4

Too quiet

I always dreaded the register being called in class: I would sit there, waiting for the moment when the teacher would read out my name; the moment when I would be expected to speak.

I was in music class one day at secondary school. I always found these classes particularly uncomfortable, because instead of sitting at desks in rows, we had to sit in a large circle, all facing each other. That day, as the teacher began calling the register, the familiar dread washed over me. When she called my name, I silently raised my hand a tiny bit, as I always did. In that moment, I couldn't speak, so this was my way of answering, of letting her know that yes, I was here. Most of the teachers were used to this; when they got to my name, they would look up, peer around the classroom, looking out for me and my raised hand. But that day, the music teacher frowned.

'You need to speak up,' she said. 'Use your voice. What if there was a fire? Nobody would be able to find you.'

When faced with this kind of situation, my default reaction was to not react. So I just continued to sit there, longing for the interaction to be over. But the other kids in the class were taken aback by the teacher's comment. Some of them spoke up: 'That's really deep, miss.' 'That was harsh.' I suppose they were trying to stand up for me, but all I wanted was for everyone to stop staring.

Then someone said, 'She's going to go cry now.'

I don't think I would have cried if they hadn't said that. But they did – and I did.

YOU'RE TOO QUIET.

YOU'RE BORING.

SPEAK UP.

DON'T YOU HAVE A VOICE?

IF THERE WAS A FIRE, NO ONE WOULD HEAR YOU.

I used to see my quietness as something to be ashamed of; something I should want to change. I wanted to be anything but quiet. Being quiet seemed to make people think I was dull, boring, stupid. That I'd burn in a fire because no one knew I existed – and it would all be my fault. I bought in to how other people viewed quietness, and believed the things they said to me.

When someone is described as quiet, it tends to conjure up the image of a mouse hiding away, terrified, in the corner. Being quiet is associated with weakness, lacking personality, lacking confidence.

Here are some things people have said to me about my quietness:

- 'You're too quiet.'

- 'Speak up.'

- 'Don't you have a voice?'

- 'You're boring.'

- And, yes: 'If there was a fire, no one would hear you.'

Ghost

I grew up with severe social anxiety, and at about the time I started secondary school, I also developed selective mutism. There are a lot of misunderstandings and misconceptions around selective mutism, particularly because of its name. 'Selective' implies that it's voluntary, that the person has a choice and 'selects' when they will and won't speak. That's not what it's like. In fact, because of this misunderstanding, some people prefer the term 'situational' mutism instead of 'selective' mutism.

There were some situations and environments in which I could speak – typically, at home, I was very talkative (and stubborn!) – and there were others in which I literally couldn't. It was like my vocal cords were frozen. I felt like I had no control over the volume of my voice, and lived in fear that it would come out too loudly. Increasingly, it didn't come out at all.

I lived in my own silent bubble, afraid not only to speak, but also to do anything that would draw any attention to me. I was careful never to change even a small aspect of my appearance. I avoided making any change to my facial expression, trying not to show any reaction, no matter what happened. I even controlled how I walked – every footstep was carefully timed so my pace never changed, always remained constant. I was called a ghost. But I needed to be a ghost, to be invisible, because I couldn't work out how I would ever fit in.

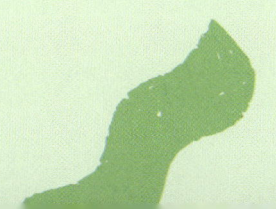

Selective mutism isn't something you choose; it's like being led to a prison by someone you trust, then, before you know it, you're locked in. The keys are on the other side of the bars, just within reach, but you're too scared to put your hands through and get them, because you don't know what else could be out there. For me, going to school every weekday and feeling constantly terrified was traumatic.

I felt like an alien. (To be honest, I still do – but these days, I'm an alien with more knowledge and strategies, and I know I am still growing and ever changing.)

So I didn't speak, and I didn't react. But I listened to everything, and I watched everyone around me interacting with each other. Part of me longed to be part of it, but part of me felt I didn't want to – because I was an alien, a ghost, a fake. I didn't feel like the other kids.

Although I was able to talk at home, things were not easy there either. Having a neurodivergent family who all had their own issues to manage compounded everything, as did growing up mixed Chinese and white/English, as I'd find myself feeling embarrassed my mum wasn't like the other mums. There was trauma in my childhood, as a result of divorce, fear and mental illness. My mum ended up bringing up three children as a single mother on benefits after my dad left for India and subsequently remarried. My home life was sometimes chaos. Though at the same time, my parents tried the best with everything they had. I'm grateful to them and everyone around me.

It wasn't until I went to university that things started to change. Because of my family's financial situation, I was eligible for the maximum bursary and grant, and it meant I was able to move away and live independently for the first time. I grabbed the opportunity with both hands, and moved to Bristol, far away from the stress that had been my norm up to that point.

I decided I was going to use all those observations of people I'd made over the years, and become the type of person who had friends and a social life. It feels strange to say that now, but back then, that's really what I'd set my mind on. I didn't go to university to learn about anything academic; I went to university to become someone who could make friends and enjoy herself. Perhaps it was the entirely new environment; perhaps it was because I was surrounded by new people who didn't know anything about me, and weren't expecting me to be that silent girl from school who never said anything – but I did it. I made friends, and I talked to people. There was an element of 'Fake it till you make it' to my approach, which by all means can be problematic, but the fresh start also helped.

Ironically, the undergraduate degree I studied was sociology – and later, my master's was in psychology. I think it's fair to say that after all those years of feeling like an alien, what I most wanted to study and try to understand was other people.

Although I am better now – despite still having (well-disguised) social anxiety – it's a misconception that selective mutism, autism or social anxiety are things people 'grow out of'. **The earlier these issues are identified and supported, the better.**

I've spoken to people whose selective mutism has continued into adulthood, or who, like me, continue to experience anxiety around social interactions.

'It's fair to say that after all those years of feeling like an alien, what I most wanted to study and try to understand was other people.'

It took me a long time to realize that my selective mutism was a result of my (suspected) autism – it came from me not understanding how to socialize with other people. My social anxiety felt somewhat rational, because I knew that I was being rejected for the way I interacted with people, and that I didn't know how to respond to them – I would often keep my face blank and simply not show any response at all. Plus, my sensory issues were compounded as I moved from primary school into the louder, busier environment of secondary school, causing me to shut down.

As I've said, I could talk at home freely. The chaos was familiar. And it sounds strange, but my younger brother and I now laugh at the fact that I often used to communicate in meows when I was at home.

Selective mutism is classified as an anxiety disorder, so having it does not mean you are also autistic – but, like me, you can have both, and there is a higher rate of anxiety disorders in people with autism. It's an under-researched area, but some studies suggest that selective mutism and autism often co-occur.

Looking back, I wish I could have changed schools, perhaps to a smaller school that was far away enough to give me a real fresh start. I think I'd also have benefited from therapy and a buddy system in that new school. What would have helped the most, though, was greater understanding. **People with selective mutism aren't being difficult or awkward or 'shy'.** They literally cannot speak in certain situations.

Even though I say I'm 'better', and despite the fact I've appeared on a big TV show, which was a real privilege because of the opportunities it has brought me, I still experience moments when I feel that fear of speaking or being perceived sneaking back in. It's nowhere near as extreme as it was before, but it still tries to crawl back sometimes, and I have to keep working at putting it back in its bin.

Quietly confident

I think growing up in the way I did is the main reason why I'm now so fascinated by the idea of trying to be my most authentic, joyful self, and how that can fit into a world that isn't always accepting of difference. I'm sharing these parts of my story because that's part of my own experience of trying to be authentically 'me'. Although selective mutism is part of my story, there will be plenty of 'quiet people' reading this who haven't had that experience. We're all different, and struggle in different ways.

People often assume that being quiet means you're introverted and lack confidence, but these are all different things, different facets of what make up a person.

Some introverts *are* quiet people – but other introverts are quite talkative, while some extroverts are naturally quiet. **Being an introvert or an extrovert has nothing to do with the volume of your voice or how often you use it**

– it's about whether you process things inwardly or outwardly, and whether you gain more energy from time spent with other people or alone. Most people are neither one nor the other, but somewhere in between or close to the middle.

It's also important to remember that just because someone is quiet, it doesn't mean they lack confidence or have low self-esteem. For example, I'm an introverted, quiet (most of the time), socially anxious person, and (these days, at least) I'm also a reasonably confident person (I must be, otherwise I wouldn't be putting this book out there!). **All these things can be true at once!** You can be both confident AND quiet. And quietly full of joy.

Take a look at the diagram below and mark with an 'x' where you think you are on each 'scale'. It's likely that your 'x' marks won't all align – and you'll probably find that their positions will move around at different times and in different situations. This can be a useful visual reminder that these things are all different.

INTROVERSION ◄----------------► **EXTROVERSION**

LOW SELF-ESTEEM ◄----------------► **HEALTHY SELF-ESTEEM**

QUIET ◄----------------► **MORE VERBALLY EXPRESSIVE**

It's worth remembering that some of the best relationships and friendships are between introverts and extroverts! We look after each other, and each bring our own unique brilliance to the table.

There's joy in being quiet – and there's also joy in being talkative, or somewhere in between, or to be different in different situations, and/or as you experience change. Although I no longer struggle with selective mutism, I still have situations where I'm quiet, and situations where I'm more vocal. Typically, I'm on the quiet side, but not all the time – sometimes I just want to talk and talk, mostly to my partner Nabil, and mostly about interior design ideas, baking inspiration, insights into my chronic health issues and mental health realizations. Sometimes I talk so much that Nabil's eyes start to glaze over, and he just nods his head along as I enthusiastically share my latest insights.

We may be quiet on the outside, but that doesn't mean we don't have loud (sometimes overly so), thoughtful, wondrous minds!

There is strength AND JOY in being quiet

I hope that by now it's clear that **being quiet – or being not quiet – is neither good nor bad. It's neutral**. Although in this section I'm going to be talking about some of the strengths and joys of being quiet, that's mainly because quiet people are often criticized or overlooked. I'm not saying that it's *better* to be quiet. It's not better; it's not worse. It just *is*. In the same way that I was criticized for being quiet when I was younger, many children are told off for being 'too loud' or called 'chatterboxes'. These terms can carry feelings of shame for a long time after we're grown. So I've tried to use neutral terms here, such as 'talkative' or 'more verbally expressive'.

'I'm not saying that it's *better* to be quiet. It's not better; it's not worse. It just *is*.'

So – there are admirable qualities about and joys of being quiet, just as there are admirable qualities about being more verbally expressive. Sometimes, quiet people get overlooked; they may not feel able to speak up and take credit for their own hard work or ideas in a meeting, or might find they get passed over when the time comes for promotions or other opportunities because they're quietly getting on with projects rather than leading conversations and being in the middle of things. While every workplace – and every school, and every social setting – benefits from both quiet and more talkative people, quiet people sometimes have to fight a bit harder to be more authentically themselves, because society is set up in a way that naturally favours those who are more vocal.

Being quiet doesn't mean you don't have great ideas. It doesn't mean you're not a valuable and hardworking member of your team, or family, or friendship group. It doesn't mean you are boring – in fact, quite the opposite! Just like the title of this book, **joy is in the ordinary**. The ordinary is often quiet; it's in the background, but it's powerful – like strong waves continually rolling in from the ocean, ebbing and flowing, quietly bringing calm to anyone watching them. Whoever you are – and however much you have to say – you have value.

People who are quiet often share many strengths (although, of course, we are all different), including:

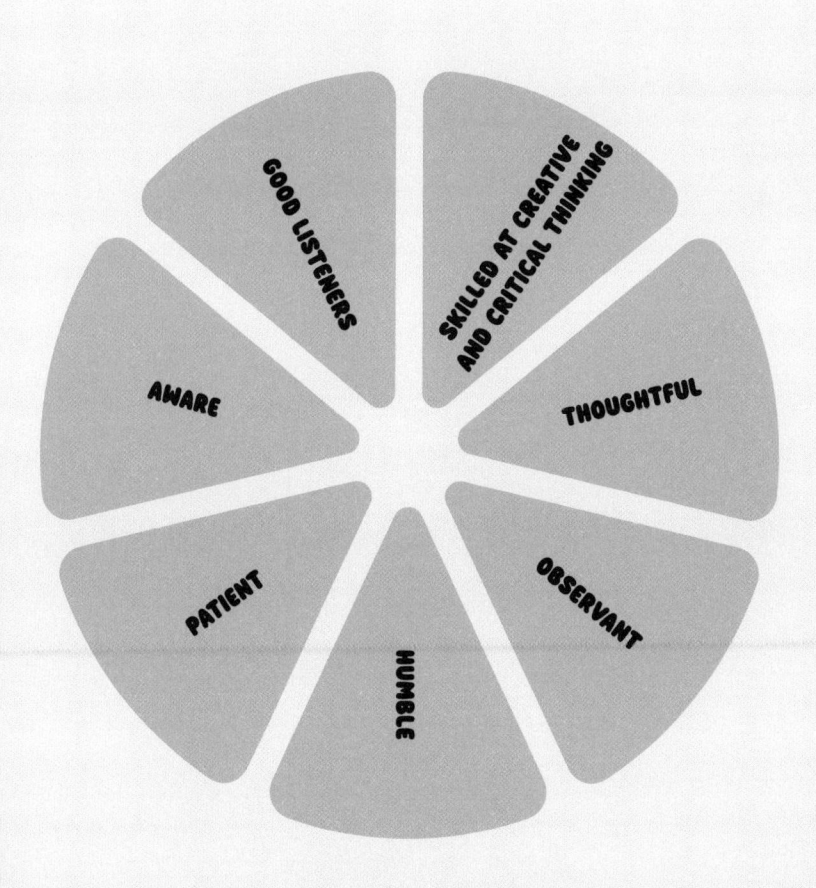

- GOOD LISTENERS
- SKILLED AT CREATIVE AND CRITICAL THINKING
- THOUGHTFUL
- OBSERVANT
- HUMBLE
- PATIENT
- AWARE

The qualities and strengths of someone who is quiet might be different to those of someone who is more chatty or vocal – but **they are equal in value**. Accept who you are – there are strengths to every side.

One of my strengths as a quiet person is that I'm a good listener. I'm comfortable with being quiet and don't feel the need to fill silences, which can create space for other people to share how they are feeling.

I was working as a support worker in the community for people with learning disabilities. One of the people I worked with was non-speaking, and part of my role was simply to sit with him and spend time together. Sometimes we watched TV; sometimes he would hand me a pen and paper and happily watch as I drew pictures. We didn't need to interact verbally in order to connect and communicate. I knew that some of my colleagues found this kind of situation challenging; they wanted to fill the quiet and chat, but that wasn't what this person wanted or needed. My natural quietness meant I was able to support him in a way that was meaningful for both of us.

In another role, I worked in an inpatient unit for people with learning disabilities. One of my colleagues there was very different to me; he was so skilled, chilled and verbally confident, and could put patients at ease with his effortless chat. I used to watch the way he interacted with patients, colleagues and visitors alike and wish I could be like that. But at the same time, some of the patients valued my quieter approach, and he and I occasionally used to swap shifts so we could bring our respective strengths to the patients who benefited most from them. It was a useful lesson, as I saw that although my skills **were** different to his, **they were** just as valuable. **We were both brilliant at our jobs, but we did them in different ways.**

The power of being quiet

If you're a quiet person, try to think of some examples of when your quietness has proven to be a strength. These can be hard to think of, especially if you have grown up in an environment that sees being quiet in a negative light, but give yourself some time and you'll be surprised.

Here are some thoughts to potentially get you going:

- Sometimes saying nothing says more than words ever could. There's a reason we are asked to be silent when paying our respects.

- If someone is being dishonest, being quiet can be a powerful response. If you don't respond verbally right away, they may attempt to fill the silence and reveal the truth.

- If someone is being unkind or negative, being quiet can enable you to protect your energy rather than engaging with their behaviour.

- Staying quiet can be a powerful response when something significant has happened. It gives you and everyone around you time to process the situation.

Being quiet in a vocal world

While we've seen that there is nothing wrong with being quiet, we do live in a world that tends to favour those who are more verbally expressive. There can be pressure to change your behaviour if you feel your natural 'quiet' self isn't appreciated.

Here are some questions to ask yourself in this kind of situation:

- **Am I playing a role or pretending to be something I'm not?** This can be hard to identify – I still sometimes find it hard to be sure whether I'm doing something because I want to or because I think it's expected of me (people-pleasing strikes again!).

- If you answer 'yes' to the question above, try to examine why you're doing this. **Are there any specific reasons you can identify?**

- You may be in a situation where you feel that pushing yourself to be more vocal is unavoidable (a workplace, for example). If so, is **there a way to squeeze more of the real you in there, so that you don't become exhausted and can still present your real, authentic self?**

It turns out I have a lot to say about being quiet! I hope this chapter has helped you understand your own quiet nature or that of someone you care about. I'll leave you on a fun note: sometimes, we quiet people find other ways than verbal expression to communicate. **I often communicate in cake**. I recently made a wedding cake for my best friends EJ and JJ – and it was the perfect way for me to express my love for them and my happiness at being part of their celebration. You can, quite literally, say it with cake.

Affirmations for quiet people

- I have quiet strength.
- There is value in my quiet calm.
- I am creative, intuitive and kind.
- I have a quiet voice and a strong soul.

'Whoever you are - and however much you have to say - you have value.'

5

Laziness doesn't exist

Growing up in England, it can feel like day after day is cloudy and grey, without much sunshine from one day to the next. But even on these gloomy days, I would come home from school with what I thought was a bad headache – with pounding pain and my eyes hurting from even the feeblest of light. My brain became foggy and felt almost like it was physically shutting down. It always got worse as the day went on. After a night's sleep, it seemed to reset to a lower, more manageable level, but then as the day wore on I'd feel that gradual decline as if my brain was powering off, while the pain simultaneously mounted. I sometimes used to joke that I must be a vampire, because I just couldn't seem to handle the daylight.

I didn't do anything about it. I pushed through every day, ignoring the signals from my body, and just tried to keep going. I mentioned it to other people, but they said (in a well-meaning way), 'Yeah, I know what you mean. I get really tired too.'

That must be it, I thought. I'm just a bit tired – I must be overreacting. Everyone gets headaches every day, right? So why am I making such a big deal out of it? They must be feeling the same way as me, but they're better at pushing through.

So I kept trying to push through, too.

TIRED
tired
tired
tired
tired
tired
tired
tired

just a bit tired

tired
tired
TIRED
tired
tire
TIRED

It took me until recently to figure it out that I've had chronic daily migraine since I was a teenager. I didn't understand that was what had been happening to me until my symptoms had worsened and become completely debilitating. I was working as a psychological wellbeing practitioner, trying to be completely present and focused for the clients I was working with, but as the days wore on and my symptoms worsened, the fog enveloped my brain. Sometimes it felt like my head was becoming unbearably hot. My light sensitivity intensified until I couldn't bear to have the overhead lights on. Ideally, I'd have drawn the curtains, too, but I couldn't sit with my clients in semi-darkness, so I kept pushing through. I didn't ask for accommodations; I didn't really know what to ask for, because I didn't understand what was happening to me.

It was a gradual progression. My morning bout of 'energy' gradually got shorter and shorter, until that 'reset' I'd always experienced after a night's sleep just ... stopped.

I reached the point where I could sleep for 12 hours, and still wake up feeling like I was only half there. And though I'm a lot better now thanks to medication, still, every day, my eyes and head hurt from the light, even with sunglasses on – and I wear them all the time, even when I'm indoors. I see static, like you might see on an old television; it's overlayed on my vision, all the time. If I turn to look at something, my head feels like it's still moving after I've stopped. I experience dizziness and lightheadedness. There's always pain in my head, face, one side of my neck and shoulders, and my muscles often feel fatigued.

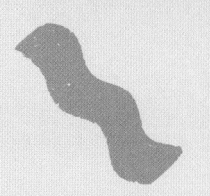

And when I try to 'push through', as I always have, it makes everything even worse. It causes mood switches, where I suddenly feel disconnected from myself, like nothing is real.

I've been seeing a neurologist, and I'm thankfully getting better – though I still experience symptoms daily – but I'm beginning to learn more about what's happening to me. My neurologist told me, 'Migraines do what they want. They don't always fit a usual pattern.'

Even now, I still underplay these symptoms. I'm only just figuring out the words to explain what's happening to me, and getting the courage to be vulnerable enough to talk about it – to shared what's really going on. Working on this book and writing down what is affecting me is helping me to do that.

My health problems mean I'm not able to work like I once did. They mean I need to sleep a lot more than some people do. They mean my whole body hurts, so when we're out and about, my partner Nabil often carries my bag for me. The brain fog that overwhelms me means that sometimes I can't get the words out that I'm looking for; I sometimes sound confused or like I'm not paying attention.

And there is a part of me that can't help sometimes feeling worried about how that looks to other people.

Oh wow, she's sleeping in again – that girl just loves a lie-in.

Taking another day off? It's alright for some, I suppose.

Oh look, her poor partner, carrying her bag for her. So lazy.

So lazy.

So. Lazy.

But there's nothing lazy about dealing with a chronic illness. I've had to really advocate for myself in order to get the help I need. I've had to spend hours, weeks, months, researching my symptoms and trying to find out where to go for help. I've been on waiting lists; I've been to countless appointments; I've tried different medications and treatments.

And do you know what else? Chronic illness or not, **I don't think 'laziness' exists**.

The laziness lie

Most of the people I've encountered have been very accommodating and understanding about my condition, and I feel lucky to be surrounded by these people. I haven't ever heard anyone outright calling me lazy to my face (or if I have, I don't remember, because my memory is so hazy – and maybe that's a blessing here!). But intentionally or unintentionally, I have experienced a lot of subtle comments that allude to the idea of laziness – the idea that I could be doing more, or that I'm somehow 'failing'.

I've shared my story from my perspective of dealing with chronic illness, but so many of us experience this feeling of being perceived as 'lazy' for countless other reasons, including mental or physical health issues, neurodivergence, lack of opportunities, financial constraints and caring responsibilities. Most of us experience barriers and challenges that can leave us feeling like we're not doing enough.

But the truth is, going through this experience has made it clear to me that **I am just as valuable as others**. Each of us can only do our best with what we're given, and we're all given different opportunities and strengths.

I don't believe a person can be simply defined as 'lazy'. **Calling someone lazy is a moral judgement.** The idea of 'laziness' in this context is entirely a cultural construct – and it's almost always used to demonize the poor, people of colour, people who are disadvantaged in life, people who are vulnerably housed, disabled people – the list goes on. It's often used as a dismissive and demeaning term to describe young people, too. Personally, I feel that 'laziness' is a symptom of a dysfunction in wellbeing. Even when we can't see a clinical condition or anything on the surface, we don't know what's going on underneath. Anyone with perceived 'laziness' should be helped, not judged and reprimanded.

'LAZY' — above the surface

below the surface:
- Trauma
- Executive function difficulties
- Chronic illness
- Caring responsibilities
- Grief
- Exhaustion
- Poverty
- Loss of identity
- Mental health issues
- Burnout
- Learned coping strategies

You've probably heard some variation on the phrase:
'We all have the same 24 hours in a day.'

We do not.

OK, in a literal sense, there are 24 hours in a day. But those 24 hours look dramatically different for each of us. Someone living with mental illness does not have the same 24 hours as someone who does not. Someone with three children does not have the same 24 hours as someone with none. The list goes on – we are all different, with different needs, responsibilities and opportunities, and each of us has a different 24 hours. But for some reason, if you don't manage to 'achieve' enough with your *24 hours*, our society is predisposed to see you as lazy.

I think of this as 'the laziness lie'. It's made up of three smaller lies:

- You can always be doing more.

- Your productivity is your worth.

- You cannot trust your own needs.

> **'We are all different, with different needs, responsibilities and opportunities, and each of us has a different 24 hours.'**

Lie number 1: 'You can always be doing more'

After trying every medicine and random online remedy, I've recently started taking a new medication, and it has brought me back to the level I was at a few years ago (it's been miraculous).

When I talked about this with my partner Nabil, he suggested that now that I'm feeling a bit better, I should keep 'doing positive things', keep taking action and trying to build on what I've managed so far so that I can keep doing more.

He was speaking from a well-intentioned place of love and support, and I understood where he was coming from: committing to keeping taking positive steps is clearly a good strategy for building your self-esteem, increasing muscle strength, energy reserves and helping with depression, and of course, I am hoping to keep doing as much as possible.

But – and it's a big but – my energy is finite. So is everybody's. **We all just max out whatever energy we have to hand**.

I have a complex neurological disease, and that's what causes my limitations. Now that my illness is better managed, the finite amount of energy I have available has expanded – but it's still finite.

Nabil's energy is finite too. Even though he is able-bodied and works a lot, he still has finite resources. He may have *more* resources than I do, but **they're not limitless**.

This diagram shoes Nabil's finite resources. The different sections show the things that take up his resources: work, socializing, personal care and hygiene, exercise and cooking, and everything else.

Nabil:

[Diagram: bar showing Nabil's resources with sections labeled Work, Other, Personal care, hygeine etc., Exercise & cooking]

These diagrams show my finite resources, both before and after managing my condition with medication – this is important, because your resources (and how they are allocated) can change over time. Before medication, my resources were very limited. Now I have more, but they're still more limited than Nabil's.

Me before I managed my condition:

[Small bar diagram]

Me now I have medication to manage:

[Medium bar diagram]

113

When I explained this, Nabil said, 'But I still think I *could* be doing more. I could be going to the gym like other people. I could be cooking healthier meals and losing weight.'

The fact that other people go to the gym and cook healthier meals doesn't mean Nabil is being lazy because he doesn't do those things. **His resources are already used up**. If you want to do more things, you either have to reallocate your resources (which is not always possible, as many of them, like work, are non-negotiable), or increase your resources (which, again, is not always possible). Everyone uses up all the resources they have available; if you give someone more resources, they do more with them. Nobody's out there lounging on a pile of resources and consciously refusing to use them.

It's hard to see this because not everyone has the same choices. And a lot of this is invisible.

For instance, someone with a healthy upbringing and stable family may look at someone with depression and say 'If I was them, I'd just go to therapy and get out of this rut!' Or to somebody in an unhealthy relationship, 'But they could just leave! I would just leave if I was them'. They may assume they can insert themselves and their life experiences into that other person's shoes. But putting on the shoes is one thing, and walking for miles in them is another. Maybe that depressed person is traumatized by a past therapy experience. Maybe that person who doesn't 'just leave' fears being alone due to past traumatic experiences. The choices that may seem obvious to other people, are not actually always available to them.

It's also important to remember that we all have different priorities and goals. Two people could have the same finite quantity of resources available to them and use them differently. Just because one doesn't focus on the same priorities and goals as the other, it doesn't mean they're lazy – they're just using their resources differently.

Increasing and decreasing resources

What increases our available resources?

Privilege (in any form), such as:

- Good mental health

- Being able-bodied and physically healthy

- Having access to education

- Being financially stable and having access to money

- Being well rested

- Living in a safe and stable environment

Having access to money, for example, can mean you are able to free up more of your time. If you can afford to pay a gardener or cleaner, you can spend less time on household tasks. If you can afford access to better healthcare, you might be able to resolve health issues faster. It turns out money *does* matter – so I'd love to win the lottery! Every Lunar New Year, my family give each other red envelopes full of money known as *ang pow*, and we say '*Kung hei fat choi*' – 'Wishing you happiness and lots of money.'

Some people will have lots of things that increase their resources, meaning their available resources, while still finite, are greater than Nabil's. There are also people who have additional responsibilities that take away from their available resources, such as parenting or caring roles (not to mention that a lot of these caring roles are unfortunately viewed as 'less productive' than going to work). Responsibilities like these mean you are left with fewer resources for yourself. For example:

Parenting →

Work →

If you like, you could draw a diagram showing your own finite resources and how they are allocated. Ask yourself:

- What are my available resources?

- How are my resources allocated? (Remember to include things such as travel time in each section! If you commute to and from work, for example, your 'work' allocation includes the time and effort it takes to get there and back.)

- What increases my resources?

- What depletes my resources?

If, like Nabil, you have a list of things you think you 'should' be doing, and you berate yourself for being 'lazy' when you don't do them, take a look at your diagram. Do you really have space for those things, or are your resources already used up?

Sowing seeds

When I say that our resources are finite, I'm not saying you should just give up; **it's about being realistic**, and a constructive way of implementing being kind to yourself. Once you understand what your own resources look like, then you can figure out what's achievable. When Nabil and I talked about this, one really positive point that came up was that even when your resources are limited, you can still sow seeds for your future. You can water them, give them the sunlight they need to grow, and show them the care they need to flourish. And you can do that while knowing your own worth, and without pushing yourself beyond your limits.

This is something I learned when my health was at rock bottom. For me, the seeds I sowed were learning how to rest (although as anyone with a chronic physical or mental illness will tell you, rest in this circumstance doesn't always feel like rest!). I had to learn to reject the impulses that were telling me to 'push through', so I could let my body and mind rest and recover. I also devoted what energy I had to researching my condition, planting the seeds that enabled me to seek the help I needed.

To be clear, the aim with sowing these seeds doesn't have to be to nurture the plants and increase your capacity just so you can go back to being a productivity machine, working excessive hours and experiencing guilt that you're still not doing *enough*, all over again. The focus is on growing your own forest to sustain and nourish you, potentially improving your resources while accepting that they are and always will be finite.

Lie number 2: 'Your productivity is your worth'

In our culture, we are constantly bombarded with both overt and subtle messages telling us that our worth is intrinsically tied to our productivity. We live in a world that values busyness and 'getting things done'. **It's hard not to internalize those societal messages** – and when you do, and you aren't able to work or participate in this culture of busyness and productivity, it can have a massive impact.

Being busy all the time is great if that's what you thrive on, but it's also the standard that everyone feels pressured to live up to, whether it works for them or not.

Recently, I've been having a lot of conversations that go a little like this:

'Hi, Kim-Joy! How are you? I bet you've been busy with your books and the house renovations.'

And sometimes I follow the ritual; it's almost like I feel I have to. I don't want to disappoint anyone. So I say, 'I'm good, thank you, how are you? Yes, I've been busy. I'm currently working on a self-help book!'

Announcing our busyness is the norm, and assuming someone else is busy can be a way of showing respect, as we're implying they are productive and therefore useful to society. But why should it always be that way? Are we not useful if we're not dashing about having meetings and sending off emails?

Sometimes, I try to challenge this by saying, 'I've just been sleeping and trying to relax'.

When I see the other person's face drop or sense that they're confused, I quickly make a joke about it, and I feel pressure to add something about my future plans to be productive: 'I haven't done much house-decorating lately, BUT I've got all these plans – look!'

I wish I didn't feel I have to do this. The truth is that some days, I'm not baking a cake and filming it for social media, because I just need to sleep.

Rest is not a reward

Rest is not something you 'get' to do when you finally reach the end of that to-do list. It's not your prize for being so busy or for having done 'enough'. Rest is not a reward: it is a need. You shouldn't feel like you have to 'earn' rest or justify it to others. We are mammals: we need food, water, warmth and rest to survive.

Lie number 3: 'You cannot trust your own needs'

So often, when we feel like we are in need of a rest or break, we don't trust these feelings. We try to ignore them, assume they are 'wrong', and tell ourselves to 'push through' or keep going so that we can get more done – and so 'earn' our rest. Instead of acting on our needs, **we act on the pressure we feel to be constantly productive**. I did this a *lot*.

What if we applied this attitude to other needs? For example, imagine that you are feeling cold, but instead of deciding to put on another layer or close the window, you tell yourself, 'I'm not really cold, I just need to keep going,' or perhaps, 'Well, I need to keep this up for at least another hour, and then I can be warm.' It doesn't make sense. So why do we ignore our needs when it comes to rest?

I spoke about this with a friend, and they said to me, 'But what about procrastination? Sometimes we say we need to take a break, but we're really just procrastinating because we are avoiding a particular task.' Procrastination is complicated.

It's not a character flaw or a sign of a lack of self-control. Instead, it's a complex coping mechanism employed for a multitude of reasons (self-doubt, frustration, perfectionism, mental health issues, boredom, resentment, to name just a few). Sometimes, we procrastinate because we really do need a break, but we feel guilty about resting. So instead of taking a meaningful rest, we procrastinate by doing something unimportant rather than the main task.

You've probably also heard of the phenomenon known as **'revenge bedtime procrastination'**, which is when we delay going to bed so we can squeeze in all the leisure activities, hobbies and self-care we've missed out on during the day because we haven't had enough free time and rest. This is definitely something I catch myself doing – but at least now I recognize it, and this helps me to schedule my day so that procrastination doesn't eat into my sleep time.

If we could reframe our attitudes towards rest and reclaim it, we might find we procrastinated less, because we would be allowing ourselves the rest we need.

The intersection of privilege and the laziness lie

I want to reiterate that there are real world constraints to trying to reclaim rest. If you have less privilege, not only do you have fewer resources to allocate to rest (and are more likely to have the laziness myth weaponized against you), but you sometimes also have to 'prove' your worth to a higher standard, simply because of the colour of your skin or your accent, or even the type of job you do. For instance, working 15 hours a week, being a carer for a relative for 10 hours a week, and doing all the housework/cooking for 10 hours a week, is often judged as being less 'productive' than someone else working a 35-hour week. Yet both of these people are working the exact same amount.

Reclaiming rest

Mindfulness and slowing down

You've probably heard about mindfulness in relation to meditation, but it doesn't have to look like that. Not everyone can meditate – I can't! For me, **mindfulness is about focusing your attention on being in the moment**, and savouring whatever it is you are doing. For example, when I have a cup of tea, I know I'm often paying more attention to thinking about what I have to do next than I am to the cup of tea in my hand. More and more, though, I'm trying to just sit there and *be*. To savour my tea, light some candles, put on my lava lamp, look at my plants and admire their new growths, taking a moment to feel grounded and cozy. That's just what works for me – you might find a different moment or ritual that grounds you. It could be anything, from washing up to sitting in the garden for five minutes. Take intentional pauses in your day and cherish them.

As you have more of these moments of mindfulness, you can try to apply the same approach in other areas of your life. Next time you're cooking, or making something, or even cleaning the bathroom, try focusing on the process, not the outcome. Pay attention to the moment that you're in now. You might find that, in time, these moments of mindfulness become seeds you can sow to increase your resources.

Get cozy

I've always said that my biggest skill is knowing how to be cozy and comfortable. It's where almost all my interests originate: baking, interior design, lighting, fluffy socks, cats, psychology, plants... They're all about comfort. I actually feel *un*comfortable when other people are not comfortable! Everywhere I go, I think about how a place could be made more comfortable. I've taught my partner Nabil to change into pyjamas when he comes home, and to enjoy the coziness of candles and a heated blanket. I'm still trying to convince him to get better socks, but he's not so bothered about that right now (which is fair enough; everyone has different comfort needs). Socks aside, he does say he loves how I've taught him how be more intentionally cozy. I consider myself a self-taught comfort expert! That might sound big-headed, but it's a real passion of mine.

Coziness and a focus on being comfortable can be associated with laziness or complacency. People talk about the need to 'get out of your comfort zone', and say things like, 'I can't get too comfortable, otherwise I won't do anything.' I disagree. Why be uncomfortable when you could be comfortable?

I think the statement of 'get out of your comfort zone' is well-intentioned but misleading – it's generally a comment on *complacency* rather than comfort. Sometimes complacency and going down a well-travelled road, but one that is not the best for you long term (like a bad relationship), can mean you're missing out on *even more* comfort. **Surely the end goal is true comfort?** Comfort isn't the same as doing nothing, it's simply the state of being where you can function as your best, joyful and authentic self.

And when it comes to resting, doing so in a cozy, comfortable environment will leave you feeling far more replenished and nourished.

What does rest look like for you?

As I keep saying, we're all different, and that means **rest looks different for everyone**. Some people find taking a long bath restful; others prefer 'active rest', like going for a jog. What does rest look like for you? Here are some possibilities, but they won't apply to everyone. Essentially, rest is anything you're doing that's not being done in order to intentionally or solely be productive.

- Taking a nap
- Watching a familiar film or TV show
- Playing a game
- Cooking
- *Not* cooking (going out for a meal!)

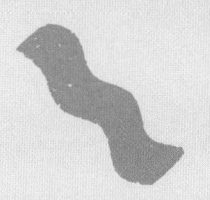

- Hanging out with your pets

- Letting yourself just 'zone out' a little

- Organizing a cupboard or drawer (again, not in order to be productive, but just to enjoy the soothing process)

- Caring for your plants

Reframing rest

Even when we are trying to look after ourselves and consciously rest, we might experience lingering feelings of guilt over being 'lazy'. So next time you are planning to have a 'lazy Sunday', or find your energy is lower and you're needing to move more slowly, try using different language. Here are some of my favourites:

- I'm having some sloth time.

- I'm focusing on being more cat.

- I'm having some zen time.

- I'm taking a goblin day.

- I'm enjoying a peaceful pause.

- I'm relishing a leisurely day.

- I'm appreciating just doing nothing.

- I'm being intentionally unproductive.

- I've scheduled a day to be quiet and calm at home.

Or you can simply say, 'I'm chilling today.' I usually use some variation of this; it's probably my go-to phrase. But from now on, I might say 'I'm intentionally chilling'!

And remember, there's no need to add, 'because I've been working so hard' or 'because I've been doing so much'. (Though I know the temptation is there because I *do* add these bits in sometimes – it's easier in the moment.)

Even in those hard, self-critical days, where you feel 'lazy', there could be glimmers of joy, and glimmers of joy in the days, weeks and years to follow. 'Be kind to yourself'.

> If you want to look more deeply into these ideas, Devon Price's book *Laziness Does Not Exist* is an excellent place to start. It really made me think about the myth of laziness and the pressure we put on ourselves.

Comfort zone

Joy   Safety

Authenticity   Rest

Complacency zone

A bad but familiar relationship

Avoiding confrontation

6

Vulnerability

'The design of it is impeccable,' said Prue, looking at my creation: a *kagekone* (a Danish pastry dish) shaped like one of my best friends, Charlotte, heading to the opera (she's a composer) in a beautiful gown.

It was week eight in a TV baking competition, and we were down to five bakers. The tent felt strangely empty.

'The design of it is impeccable,' Paul said. 'I mean, it's very, very good. However...'

The weight of that 'however' landed with a dull thud, and I listened as they (kindly) explained the issues with my bake. The pastry had lost its butter; it was soggy; the whole thing was underproved.

I nodded, taking in their feedback, knowing they were right, yet still feeling tears sting my eyes. I tried to blink them away, and found I could barely speak, the words catching on sobs that wanted to escape from my throat.

As Sandi helped me pick up my bake and take it back to my work station, I managed to squeak out a 'thank you'.

HOWEVER

HOWEVER

HOWEVER

HOWEVER

HOWEVER

HOWEVER

HOWEVER

HOWEVER

HOWEVER

Crying in public has always been one of my worst fears, and I know it is for many other people too. It's right up there with nightmares about suddenly giving birth to kittens (though that wouldn't really be that bad), or desperately needing a wee in public and being unable to find a toilet. I always felt like if I cried, everyone would know how much I cared, how hurt I was, how sensitive I am. They'd dismiss me as babyish – or worse, they would think I was doing it to manipulate them, that I was faking it.

But now, when I look back at those mortifying times when I 'slipped up' and cried in front of someone else, I see them in a different light.

The time I cried in front of the most people was when I cried on a massive TV show (*The Great British Bake Off*) in front of millions of viewers – and I was crying over a pastry. A PASTRY. (Albeit it was also a representation of one of my best friends.) It's very funny now.

In fairness, it was week eight of filming. I was physically exhausted, and emotionally vulnerable.

Regardless, I am and always have been extremely sensitive to criticism. Not in all situations – if someone gestured rudely to me from their car for driving at two miles per hour below the speed limit, it wouldn't bother me at all (if anything, I'd be one of those annoying people who intentionally smiles instead). But yes, I'd probably cry if you told me my cake was soggy. And I'd probably rage-cry if I knew someone was intentionally trying to make me feel bad about something (which isn't what Paul and Prue were doing, of course). And then I'd cry even more because I'd be frustrated with myself for crying.

I've always berated myself for being like this, but you know what?

I am sensitive. And that's OK.

The tears didn't come because I was weak; the tears came because I was *vulnerable*. As Brené Brown says, being vulnerable doesn't make us weak. Instead, it's a mark of true bravery. (If you're not familiar with Brené Brown, I strongly recommend checking out her books and talks on vulnerability – they helped me a great deal with understanding my own.)

I wasn't being weak when I cried on *Bake Off*. In fact, it took courage – a lot of courage – to take part in a TV show where my self-taught baking skills would be judged in front of millions.

I cried because I cared. I'd decided to apply to the show despite my social anxiety, because baking was my passion and I wanted to share it. I could have just not applied for the show in the first place, and avoided this altogether – but then where would I be?

And that example I gave of the 'cool' me in the car who doesn't get visibly upset? That's because *that* situation isn't something that makes me vulnerable – it's not a situation where I'm facing any fears. That's why I can just not care. For some people, being sworn at by another motorist would make them feel really upset. The situations that make *you* feel vulnerable are unique to you.

That moment when I found myself crying on TV is a very literal and visible example of vulnerability, but in everyday life, vulnerability can come in so many different forms, and it often goes unrecognized. **Many of us are vulnerable every single day**. Sometimes that's because we have no choice, and sometimes it's because we are working towards something.

You could be vulnerable because you are being honest about your needs, perhaps dropping some of your usual masks and armours and safety behaviours (e.g. perfectionism) in order to ask for help, admit mistakes and share how you're feeling. All these things – and many more – can make you feel uncertain, like you're taking a risk. It can feel like jumping when you can't see the ground and hoping you'll land safely, or that someone will be there to catch you.

Crying is just one sign of vulnerability. Maybe you're not someone who cries, but you might retreat or feel scared or angry, sad or frustrated. These emotions often arise because you've had the courage to put yourself in a situation where you're vulnerable.

I've used crying as an example here simply because it's so visible, and it's also an example through which you can see how society reinforces the connection between vulnerability and weakness by associating crying with childishness or immaturity. We've all heard phrases such as:

- 'Babies cry, not adults.'
- 'She's just crying to get attention.'
- 'Don't be such a cry-baby.'
- 'Only girls cry.'

(This last one is particularly upsetting: boys are told not to cry even when they're still children, because unfortunately 'weakness' is associated with femininity – although that's a whole other topic. The stigma around crying affects us all.)

Honestly, after I'd cried on the show, I was expecting to hear comments like the ones above. I even convinced myself that people would think I'd *pretended* to cry in order to get through to the next round (if that were true, forget baking and writing – I should have a career in acting). But then the episode aired, and 99 per cent of the comments were overwhelmingly empathetic and kind. There's always the loud minority, and those unpleasant comments were in there, but they were drowned out by the kindness.

That taught me a valuable lesson. Vulnerability is a sign of strength: it shows you have the courage to be authentically yourself – and this allows other people to see you. The *real* you. **It's a bridge for connection.** When people saw me crying on the show, most of them didn't judge me; instead, it felt like a point of connection, because they could all think of a time when they too had felt so overwhelmed or scared or sad that they felt the mask break and the emotions escape.

Finding strength in vulnerability

When we're used to seeing vulnerability as an indication of weakness, it can be hard to get away from this attitude. But the truth is, vulnerability can be incredibly powerful. I once defeated a bully (slight exaggeration for fun – but it's for real) – and I didn't do it by fighting them or shouting or taking revenge. I did it by crying.

> 'Vulnerability is a sign of strength: it shows you have the courage to be authentically yourself – and this allows other people to see you. The real you.'

Years before *Bake Off*, when I was at a stage in my life when I would never have applied for a TV show – I had low self-esteem, and was deeply anxious and very quiet – I started a new job. I was working as a care assistant in a care home. It was a challenging work environment; as is so often the case unfortunately, the care home was seriously understaffed, the workers were underpaid, and we all had more work to do than we could manage. I was extremely conscious of the need to do a good job. I was determined to avoid making mistakes, to blend in with everyone else and not draw attention to myself.

But she noticed me anyway.

Amanda was a cleaner at the home. She was a strong character, known for her regular shouting matches with the care-home manager. And however hard I tried to slip under the radar, Amanda saw me. Every day, she would make snippy comments at me, criticizing my work, my behaviour – my very existence, it felt like. I'd see a little triumphant smile cross her face as she noticed how I reacted to her jibes, with apologies and dismay, and a sense of disappointment in myself. She and the other cleaner would smirk at me and put me down, and then, as I walked away, they'd talk to each other about how useless I was, in voices loud enough for me to hear. It was very blatant, textbook stuff. She knew what it was, and I knew what it was.

This continued every day for around two months. As I started to get more confident in my role, I began to notice that Amanda wasn't only doing it to me. This was obviously awful, but it made me realize that her behaviour was nothing to do with me or the way I did my job, and everything to do with her. That knowledge gave me strength.

So one day, after she criticized me for not making a bed perfectly, I decided I had to say something.

When I'd imagined standing up to her in my head, I'd pictured myself standing there, strong and straight-faced, telling her in a calm yet assertive voice that her behaviour was inappropriate. In reality, of course, when the moment came, I had a tear creeping down my cheek, and I could barely get my words out because my voice was shaking so badly. All I really managed to croak out was a very broken up: 'Why do you need to make me feel bad?'

It didn't look or sound at all like the image I'd had in my head of a brave, strong me asserting herself.

But after that, Amanda stopped. Every day I'd wait for her comments and jibes, but they didn't come. She backed off. And then she started making small talk with me. She started smiling at me, but these were kind and friendly smiles, not the triumphant smirks she'd always delivered when she realized she had an opening to criticize me. She even started COMPLIMENTING me. When I left that job, Amanda was the one who organized for everyone to get me a leaving present. The dynamic had changed completely. It felt bizarre.

It was such a strange situation, but I still genuinely think that the tears and pure emotion I displayed – things I'd always thought of as a hindrance, which would make me seem weak – were what made my message stronger. Standing up to Amanda was a big thing, but showing emotion also seemed to connect me with her on some level. In that moment, I truly felt like I'd opened my heart, and she'd seen something there that she could relate to.

As much as it would feel more straightforward and simple to see every bully as a pure villain like in a superhero movie, the truth is that Amanda was a complex and struggling character, just like each of us. She was working with a manager with whom she had a tumultuous relationship, in a high-pressure, poorly paid job where her work often went unappreciated because everyone was so busy.

This is not to say that her behaviour was OK, or that bullying or bad behaviour from others is something for you to fix. **Empathizing with where people are coming from doesn't mean accepting how they impact you.** There's only so much you can do. You deserve kindness, and you aren't responsible for other people's bad behaviour and unresolved issues.

I want to be clear about something. When I said earlier that I defeated her by crying, that wasn't my plan. I wasn't *pretending* to cry to disarm her. I didn't *want* to cry. And I wouldn't recommend *trying* to cry at your bullies. But if tears happen in the process of you standing up to them, so what? Tears are a natural thing. Some of us cry easily; some of us don't. Crying can help us to process the overwhelming emotions of difficult situations. Tears can sometimes feel like a turning point. In the same way that the air feels fresh after it's rained, crying helps us to process information, heal, and sometimes see things differently.

In short, **crying is nothing to be ashamed of**.

It would be fun, though, if every bully could be defeated through the power of tears.

Connection and trust
The sense of connection that vulnerability can create – whether we're watching someone cry on a TV show, or realizing how strongly a person feels about something when they express themselves – can be deeply powerful. In personal relationships, it can help to build trust, because when we're being vulnerable, we're being genuinely ourselves. It's not a linear thing; it's more

like a cycle. Being vulnerable builds trust, which helps you find connection, which helps you feel safe in being genuinely yourself and vulnerable. And on it goes.

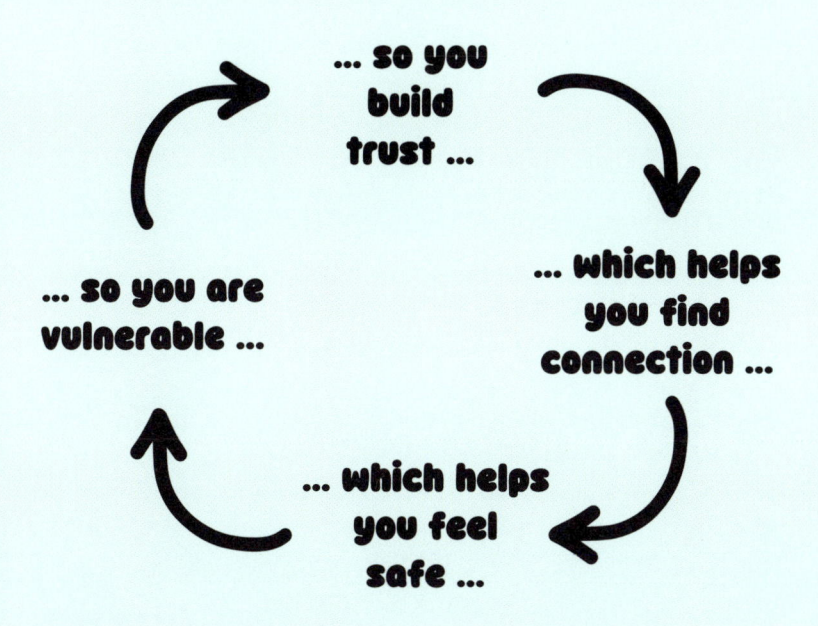

... **so you build trust** ...

... **which helps you find connection** ...

... **which helps you feel safe** ...

... **so you are vulnerable** ...

You can't be vulnerable all the time

Vulnerability is a sign of strength, plain and simple. Showing my emotions on TV and speaking up for myself when I was being bullied by Amanda both brought me strength. In different ways, the vulnerability I expressed in these situations allowed me to be more 'me'. It connected me with other people and myself. I have learned so much from being vulnerable, and it's been one of the most important things on my journey to truly connecting with who I am.

But there are some challenges and caveats here. You can't *always* be vulnerable, and there are barriers to vulnerability that will affect each of us differently. What further feeds into this is that, as we saw earlier, society has negative assumptions and double standards about vulnerability. Sometimes, we all have to play the game of pretending to be 'strong' (in the way society sees strength) in order to navigate our way through the world. **It's absolutely OK to not feel ready or not want to be vulnerable!** It depends on your unique circumstances.

Being vulnerable is also emotionally exhausting, and moments of vulnerability need to be balanced with recovery. We each have our own 'vulnerability battery'. This battery can run low, and needs to be charged up by love or having a rock (some kind of security) to run back and hide behind in case the situation and emotions become too depleting.

As I said, when I was working in the care home, there was no way I would've applied to be on a TV show. At that time, my battery for vulnerability was drained by having to be vulnerable every day. As well as that moment of extra vulnerability in standing up to Amanda, I was battling my social anxiety and worries about doing a good job every single day, and my battery was not getting refuelled by a strong support system that I could return to for validation and comfort – this all took place at the time I was house-sharing with strangers I was avoiding (see page 44), and I was struggling with family. There wasn't much in the way of a 'rock' to hide behind – what little 'rock' I had mostly comprised some good friendships.

When I applied for *Bake Off*, however, I had a robust support system, and a much larger 'rock', because I'd been living with my partner Nabil for two years or so. **I had a space of my own in which I could thrive**. I had the same level of courage back when I was showing up every day to work at the care home as I did when I applied for *Bake Off*. It was just that in the latter situation, my battery was recharged more and depleted less.

The point I want to make is that your level of vulnerability when doing one thing can't be compared to someone else's, even if they're doing the same thing. **Your battery is completely different**. It's got different fuel, it's got different configurations and needs, and it's drained by some things more than others.

Vulnerability can't be forced

Vulnerability is not a competition or something to demand or expect from others, either. I love the TV show *RuPaul's Drag Race*. In it, RuPaul sometimes asks the finalists to talk to their younger selves and give them advice, and also to talk about their inner saboteur. For some of them, this can be really positive and create a sense of connection, but for others, it can feel like they are being put under pressure to artificially generate this vulnerability. Some of the contestants don't want to speak about their traumas – maybe they're not ready, maybe it's not the right place or the right time – and that is absolutely OK. Having boundaries and saying no to being vulnerable is always OK.

Vulnerability means sharing and connecting **because you want to**, not because someone else makes you feel like you have to. This doesn't mean that all situations designed to manufacture vulnerability are problematic. Some people find it helpful to schedule time to speak with loved ones and share. Vulnerability does often happen without obvious intention, but intention is powerful. You can use intention to:

- Be mindful (*How am I feeling?*)

- Intentionally reflect (*Is this the right time and place for me to share?*)

- Give yourself compassion (*It's OK if I cry or need to ask for support.*)

- Think about what your battery looks like (*Have I got the resources I need to recharge later?*)

On the flip side, it's also important to respect other people's boundaries when you're opening up and being vulnerable. Not everyone is receptive, for various reasons. You might be trying to talk about something they find difficult themselves, or it might be that they don't have the emotional bandwidth to support you in the conversation in that moment. I often struggle to figure out what other people expect or need from me, so I will just say, 'Can I talk to you about _____? If not, that's totally OK with me.'

Comfort zone

The phrase 'Get out of your comfort zone' sometimes pops up in relation to vulnerability (we talked about this more in the chapter five) — the idea is that you need to get out of your comfort zone to be vulnerable. In some ways, this is true, but my issue, as I mentioned before, is the implication that comfort can somehow be bad. True comfort and having your needs met recharges your battery, and so enables you to be vulnerable in the first place. Comfort is needed.

Safety first

People often (but not always) respond well to vulnerability when it's something that they can relate to, that makes them think about their own experiences. My example of crying on *Bake Off* is an easy one – so many people relate to crying. But many people do not relate to or understand the difficulties faced by marginalized groups and people with differences, such as people with learning disabilities. For instance, people who have never experienced a meltdown may feel anger or discomfort in the presence of someone having one, rather than feeling empathy and connection.

Many people have good and kind intentions, and mostly *are* seeking connection. But unfortunately, that's not true for everyone. Abuse is a very real danger and the reality is that we can't be trusting of everyone. We each have a window of people who can be trusted with our vulnerability, and outside of that, people who *shouldn't* be trusted with it. Sadly, if you are disabled, mentally ill or otherwise marginalized, that window becomes smaller, as the risk of having vulnerabilities exploited is higher.

It can be hard and it may take a long time to find the people you can really trust, but they do exist.

Rejecting myths about vulnerability

Writing this chapter has been cathartic for me, and helped me reflect and piece together a lot. I hope it's been helpful for you too. Being vulnerable is one of the bravest things you can do.

But that doesn't mean we don't still have internalized negative messages about it. I still catch myself thinking that showing frustration or crying is somehow 'bad', and I have to keep challenging these thoughts with what I know is the reality. Here are some common myths about vulnerability – and the truth about those myths. See if any of them speak to you, and whether you can come up with some more of your own.

Myth: *Vulnerability is a sign of emotional instability.*

Truth: As we've seen, we're most able to be truly vulnerable when we have a good support network and are at a place in our lives where we can be authentically ourselves.

Myth: *Showing vulnerability is childish and weak.*

Truth: Being vulnerable takes strength and courage.

Myth: *Being vulnerable means sharing all your secrets.*

Truth: Trying to force someone to be vulnerable doesn't work. You can assert boundaries while still being vulnerable, and you have the right to share as much or as little as you choose (as long as the person you're sharing with is in a position to listen – see page 145). Nobody is less than or better than for being more or less vulnerable.

Myth: *It's OK for women to be vulnerable but not men.*

Truth: It's unfortunate that society tends to associate weakness with femininity, and there is often a belief that men should not express emotions. All of us can learn a great deal from being vulnerable, regardless of gender.

Go forth and be vulnerable

Vulnerability is a risk. Rejection can happen; you can feel hurt or embarrassed if sharing your emotions doesn't go the way you want it to. To be honest, the power of vulnerability wouldn't be what it is if the possibility of disappointment wasn't there. It's like saying 'I love you' to someone for the first time, when you don't know if they're going to say it back. It can feel uncomfortable to be vulnerable, but if you look back at the times in your life when you've felt real joy, the times when you've grown and become stronger and more 'you', you'll see they often stem from the times when you've been vulnerable.

'Being vulnerable is one of the bravest things you can do.'

7

Being childlike

I've loved colour ever since I was little. I own a beautiful fluffy pink-and-green coat. It's one of my favourite items of clothing, because it's soft and cozy and vibrant. Recently, I was sitting on the train, with my colourful coat covering me like a blanket. A little girl passing with her mum stopped and looked at me curiously. She said, 'Do you bring your blanket with you everywhere?'

It was such a cute moment, and I was just answering her question when her mum turned and shouted down the train, 'Come ON!'

The curiosity and wonder faded from the little girl's face, and she quickly scurried away.

Her mum hadn't done anything wrong; she was probably in a rush, probably had a million and one things to do. Perhaps we were getting close to their stop and she was worried they'd miss it. But I thought it was a shame that the little girl hadn't been able to stop and enjoy a moment of curiosity. It reminded me of how important it is to try to find space for those childlike moments of joy and wonder that can bring little pops of brightness into our days.

Immature   Uncool

CHILDISH

Babyish

                    Play
Joy   **CHILD-LIKE**
          Curiosity

Sensible   Mature

GROWN-UP

Serious

While my childhood involved a lot of tough times, it also involved a lot of adventure and play. I was obsessed with video games; I had a doll's house that I loved to rearrange and decorate; I had dozens of plushies, and I invented characters for them all and made them 'fight' each other like they were Pokémon. My brother and I made swords from sticks we'd found in the garden, as well as bows and arrows, and spent hours inventing fantasy worlds in which we were warriors and adventurers. I even made my own card game once by cutting up my dad's *New Scientist* magazines (he was not pleased about this).

But when I was a teenager, I went through a phase where I felt like I had to shed all these childlike interests. I still enjoyed video games, but I stepped away from playing in other ways. I stopped expressing myself with colourful outfits, and tried to be 'sensible' and 'grown-up'. I think part of this was because when I started secondary school, it felt a bit like everything had changed overnight; the things I had once enjoyed were suddenly deemed babyish and 'uncool', and I felt a pressure to conform with what others were doing. I think most people experience this to some extent, but I found that it made me unhappy. I wasn't really being 'me'.

Luckily for me, I quickly grew out of this phase. It sounds strange to say I 'grew out' of trying to be more 'grown-up', but I think most of understand that feeling. I recognized that embracing colour and play and cuteness and curiosity allowed me to express myself as an adult, just as it had when I was a child. I started collecting plushies again, and I still take great comfort in them today. I learned to make origami creatures. Now, I love to express myself in colour, both in my clothing and in my home, and enjoy incorporating cute elements into my interior design, like a giant Miffy lamp, magical lighting and galaxy projectors. I love video games. I enjoy creating cute characters when I'm baking and telling stories through my bakes – and this is what took me all the way through to the finals of *The Great British Bake Off*. I love to be playful in my designs; I love to learn new things and be curious. I enjoy sitting on the floor, exploring my imagination and taking delight in the little things. I love balloons – I find them kind of mesmerizing – although I can't deal with it if they pop. I consider myself to be a big child, but at the same time, I feel like an adult – and also an old lady. And the people I most enjoy being around see themselves in that way too!

We can find so much joy by embracing a more childlike approach to life – but I always think about why we so often feel we shouldn't do this. Why did I ever think that being joyful and 'me' was a bad thing? How can we find ways to bring a childlike joy back into our lives?

What's holding you back?

You can probably remember a moment during your childhood when you were told by a caregiver, teacher or other adult to 'grow up'. From a young age, we are told 'Don't be a baby,' 'Stop being so childish,' or 'It's time to be a big boy/girl.' The worst one is probably 'Act your age' – especially as it's often applied to literal children who, by playing or being curious, **are in fact very much acting their age**. As children, many of us were praised for being 'grown-up' and displaying 'mature' behaviour and criticized for more childlike play. Is it any wonder that we learned to feel a little ashamed of our childlike tendencies, and started to push them away?

It's probably useful to draw a distinction between 'childlike' and 'childish'. All too often, the two are conflated (sometimes unintentionally, and other times it's an intentional misunderstanding – see chapter nine), but while being 'childish' can mean behaving in an immature and thoughtless manner, being 'childlike' is very different.

Childlike traits

- Playfulness
- Curiosity
- Emotional expressiveness
- Wanting to learn

- Taking joy in small things
- Openness
- Sense of wonder
- Vulnerability (see the 'Vulnerability' chapter)

Childish traits

- Immaturity
- Blaming others
- Bullying
- Lack of reflection
- Not thinking of other people

Many criticisms of 'childlike' play are more focused on the traits listed above as 'childish' – it's completely possible to embrace a childlike sense of joy without being selfish, neglecting responsibilities or treating others unkindly. You can be both mature and childlike – and it can be a joyful and freeing way to be.

As I write this, I'm sat once again with that same pink-and-green coat on my lap, the one that sparked off this whole chapter, and wondering, why do so many of us lose our love for what brought us joy as children when we grow into adults?

In part, it's natural for our interests to evolve and change as we grow – for example, I don't make swords out of sticks any more (although I met someone recently at a signing who told me he still does as an adult, and I loved that, because WHY NOT? Why not do whatever you want as long as it's not hurting anyone?).

But it's not just that – there's so much more. It's so multifaceted, but here are some of the factors that repeat time and time again when people criticize an interest or behaviour that is considered 'childlike'.

Gender roles: 'That's for girls'

All hobbies are genderless, but society does label some as more feminine or masculine. And, generally speaking, the more 'masculine' the hobby, the more acceptable it tends to be. More stereotypically 'feminine' hobbies and interests, such as collecting plushies or dolls, or decorating with glitter and colour, are viewed negatively, whereas more stereotypically masculine interests, such as playing video games and sports, are more acceptable – but when you really examine it, the masculine activities aren't any less childlike. One example of this I find particularly striking is around dolls and action figures. If an adult collects dolls, it's often viewed as a bit odd – a strange and childish hobby. But if an adult collects action figures from their favourite superhero comics or movies, it's less likely to be viewed in the same way. The dolls are seen as toys for children; the action figures are considered collectors' items. But why? In both instances, the people are collecting. What makes one collection more valid than the other?

This affects everyone – cis, trans, non-binary, everyone. Childlike interests deemed more 'feminine' are discouraged, even from a very young age. If a girl expresses an interest in sport, martial arts or action films, she is likely to be praised and seen as strong and admirable, but boys are often heavily discouraged from expressing interest in things such as ballet or dolls – or anything pink. Gender is applied to play from a young age, even though many caregivers go to great lengths to avoid doing so. And later in life, it often means that certain childlike activities are even more likely to be dismissed.

Productivity: 'What's the point?'

This factor ties in to chapter five. In short, we live in a society that values productivity, and so often we think that unless we're being productive, we're failing. The impact of this on childlike interests is twofold. First, because we prioritize work and busyness, we often feel like we don't have time for play. This can be true: many people have so many work and caregiving responsibilities that there is very little space in their lives for anything else – there is no 'choice' but to prioritize these things. The second aspect of this attitude is that childlike play, by its very nature, tends not to be 'productive'. Its purpose is typically the enjoyment of the activity itself, not the outcome of the activity. Because our play activites might not leave us with something tangible or 'useful' at the end, we can feel a sense of shame around devoting time to them when we feel we 'should' be doing something else.

In my case, I struggle with the urge to turn every hobby or interest of mine into work. I feel such a pressure to film everything I create for content on social media. But sometimes the process of filming myself creating takes spontaneity and experimentation out of the experience. Every action has to be carefully crafted to look good on camera. I want to bake without filming it sometimes, but then there's always a little part of my brain that tells me I'm being 'unproductive' and wasting time. But I do intentionally try to tackle that voice: I tell it to back off and just let me *be* – let me do a chaos bake where I chuck freeze-dried blackberries plus cardamom into a batter and bake it up in a Bundt tin, not knowing where it's going to go in terms of decorating, but enjoying the chaos anyway... then deciding it has to have a rosewater drizzle and some fresh blackberries. Maybe some little faces on the blackberries. Who knows? It could taste delectable; it could taste bad. But it's all just fun.

But childlike hobbies and play are not a means to an end – they are ends in themselves. **The 'point' of these activities is simply to do them, and enjoy the experience**. To feel joy. This attitude around productivity is particularly and unfairly applied to less privileged people. We all have different privileges, but people of colour, disabled people and people from poorer backgrounds are often judged more harshly for enjoying hobbies and activities not deemed useful or productive. In the same way as the idea that rest must be 'earned', as discussed in chapter five, our society can be more forgiving or accepting of people enjoying more childlike or 'frivolous' hobbies if they are higher earners or come from a more privileged background – essentially anything that is associated with being a productive member of society.

It's as if being and/or appearing productive earns you tokens that you can spend on being childlike. And if you spend time on being childlike without first earning these tokens? Well, that's seen as spending what's unearned – you're in debt, and you face all the judgement that comes with that.

Lack of time

This one applies to most of us, to different extents, but it is still always a big factor to consider. If you have a lot of responsibilities and obligations, it might feel impossible to make space for childlike wonder. We have so much more to deal with as adults – even though our inner child wants to sneak into the kitchen, raid the cupboards, throw snowballs at our enemies, and hide in a blanket fort. Unfortunately, raiding the kitchen doesn't work, because you're the one who will have to clean it up, which is not exceptionally fun. Throwing snowballs at your enemies may land you in bigger trouble now you're an adult. And while you're in your blanket fort, your boss will call up and demand you get out. You may not be in a position to devote whole chunks of time to a revived childhood hobby or to spend time being curious and learning, but there can still be ways to bring a sense of playfulness into your life. **Think about where there are gaps in your life where you could sneak in small moments of childlike joy**. They can be tiny things, like having your morning coffee in a mug that makes you smile. Instead of a blanket fort, you could maybe just take a moment to enjoy sitting in your own cozy spot, surrounded by things you love to look at. There are further small ideas on pages 168-172.

Expectations of others
It is the expectations and attitudes of others, whether they are parents/caregivers, teachers or our peers, that tend to cause us to set aside our more childlike behaviours in the first place, alongside societal pressures. Although this is hard to navigate when we are children or in our teens, as adults, we can learn to know ourselves a little better and identify the situations in which the expectations of others do not need to affect how we behave. You may be required to dress or behave in a certain way for work, but **there can still be other areas of your life where you can embrace the joy of a more childlike approach**. Perhaps you are required to wear a uniform or follow a dress code at work – but when you get home, could you change it up to feel more 'you'? I always change into colourful, comfortable pyjamas that let my body move freely and feel like a hug all at the same time (and I'm not even a hugger – this version for me is better).

Self-consciousness
This is a big one for a lot of people, and it ties into the point above. Adopting a more childlike and playful approach can make us very visible, and if you struggle with feelings of self-consciousness or low self-esteem, it could really put you off. Having been there, I get it. It will be different for you as an individual, but I firmly believe that there will be ways and means to let you embrace the moments of joy without getting that 'too exposed' feeling. There is no 'right' or 'wrong' way to do this. You do you.

Upbringing and education

As a child, if you were praised for being 'grown-up' and told off for being 'babyish' or asking questions, it's possible you may have internalized this and view more childlike behaviours negatively. Similarly, our education can have a lasting impact on how we view playfulness and creativity. If you were taught in a way that prioritized academic achievement and learning by rote rather than experimenting and discovering, **it can take time and effort** to unlearn these beliefs and allow yourself a more playful approach.

You are probably already aware of the above on some level, but hopefully this helps chuck it out in the open. As always, knowledge is power. It will hopefully allow you to place less guilt on yourself, and instead fuel getting more of that inner-child joy through the gaps between the barriers. (I will talk about this more further into this chapter).

Too often, guilt and negative self-talk is used as the driver for change – thoughts like: *My friend/partner/colleague is so much more spontaneous and joyful than me* and *I'm not trying hard enough*, and so on. But when you have those thoughts, why not use curiosity and kind self-talk as a driver for change instead? *My friend/partner/colleague is very spontaneous and joyful and I admire that in them. I wonder what it is in their life that enables them to be like that? Could I encourage more of that in my life?*

There are certain things you can't change (for example, your upbringing or your ethnic background), but there is plenty you can do to gradually encourage yourself to welcome more childlike joy. It's also OK to feel negative too; it's normal. Being childlike is not static. After all, children are never just happy all the time. Personally, I have mood shifts that occur as part of my chronic migraine – they aren't caused by the pain, they are caused by the neurological changes in my brain. Many days I feel very gloomy. I don't feel curious, I don't want to try new things, I don't feel very childlike. I want to eat ice cream and have a nap and do nothing else. But when I really think about it, **that is childlike**. It's childlike to feel your emotions and let yourself have that ice cream and that nap you need. And deep down, I am lucky enough to know that there are better days to come.

Questions to ask yourself

As a child

- Were you praised for being 'grown-up'?

- Were you taught in a way that restricted curiosity?

- Were you told not to ask questions?

- Did you have a lot of responsibilities from a young age, such as chores or caring responsibilities?

- Were you ever made to feel that your interests were 'babyish', or that you should have outgrown them before you were ready?

As an adult

- Do you feel like there is literally no space or time for play in your life?

- Do you feel a pressure to behave in a certain way, perhaps because you have to be a role model or because of the job you do?

- Do you feel self-conscious about bringing childlike elements into your life? Why?

- How do you feel when you see children playing? Think about the answers you gave to the questions above – do you see children playing and think they should grow up, or do you see the joy and excitement they are experiencing?

Depending on how you most enjoy exploring ideas, you could try journaling or doodling based on the questions above. See what comes up for you.

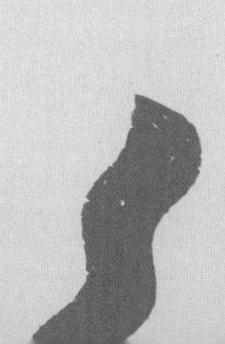

Bringing back a sense of childlike joy

Recently, I was on a trip to York. It had been a long day and I wasn't looking forward to getting in the car to go back home. But as we walked down The Shambles, we came across a long queue of people. I was intrigued and stopped to look. Most of the people in the queue were adults; they were all different ages and from different backgrounds. The thing they had in common was that they were all VERY excited.

So, on an impulse, we decided to join the queue, even though we didn't know what it was for. Before long, a man dressed in a Victorian costume came and told us that they were closing the queue – we were the last people allowed to join. It felt like fate. No way could we leave the queue now. I found out that we were in a line to visit the York Ghost Merchants, a shop selling adorable little ghost ornaments with tons of unique designs. People love collecting them, and queue for ages to enjoy the experience of visiting the store. When we got to the front of the queue, we entered a magical space filled with these tiny, beautiful ghosts. The staff were all in costumes, and everyone seemed enchanted by their surroundings. I chose my ghost and paid for it, and then the staff member who was helping me placed the ghost on a tiny train that was running along tracks around the length of the shop. I watched as my little ghost took a train ride to the shop's exit, where it was packaged up and handed to me. I was so glad I'd decided to be spontaneous and playful and join that mysterious queue.

OK, I probably joined that line partly because of the fear of missing out and the British-ness of being drawn to a queue, but a friend pointed out to me that it was more about childlike play. My experience that day reminded me of **how magical it can be just to be open, spontaneous and curious about new experiences**, and it was also a nice example of how childlike behaviours – collecting, dressing up, enjoying cute or pretty things – can be just as valuable and enjoyable for adults as they can for children.

So far this chapter has been about figuring out what has been holding you back from experiencing childlike joy. Once you've figured out those barriers, you can move on to the exciting stuff – looking at the gaps where you can bring in more of your childlike self. I love this bit. I personally keep revisiting these questions and seeing how I can bring in more of the childlike 'me'.

Here are a few questions to consider (these could be identifying what you already do, or maybe thinking about where you could introduce a bit more joy):

- What are your barriers to being childlike?

- What did you really love doing as a child?

- What was your favourite toy or game, and why?

- Is there spontaneity in your life?

- How do you feel about making mistakes?

- How do you feel about learning/being curious?

- Do you experience wonder in the little things?

- How vulnerable do you allow yourself to be? (see also chapter six)

- Do you let yourself experience a range of emotions?

- As an adult, are there any little moments in your day that bring you a burst of joy?

And note that being 'childlike' can look very different for you personally. Some of the below examples are specific to working through common barriers, and some are fun, generalized examples:

- **It could look like enjoying similar activities to those you did as a child** (but perhaps slightly upgraded now that you have the independence and possibly – yay! – the money to go even further with them). So if you used to love building and making things, why not get a Lego set or something similar that works for you. You can lose yourself in that magical flow state, when you're entirely focused on making something purely for the sake of making it.

- **If judgement from others is a barrier, how could you reduce that or work around it?** This is a tricky one, because as mentioned before, society doesn't approve when our childlike interests appear to exceed what our productivity grants us. (This very much ties into chapter five.) As an example, I really struggled last year when my chronic migraine became very disabling and I could barely work. I didn't want to be judged for staying in bed because that's what my inner child needed more than anything. My strategy was to surround myself with people who understand me (as much as people possibly can), to stay curious and focus on what treatments could make me better, to find those small moments of joy and really savour the moment, stay colourful and bright with my clothing, and keep remembering the mantra: my productivity is not my worth. But honestly? I also tried to give the illusion of productivity somewhat – by talking about my plans for the future, downplaying how I felt. It feeds society a bit of what it wants and keeps the judgement off you. Of course it's not ideal, but if you're struggling and can't work, and all you have energy to do is play video games or do some gardening for your mental health, you will know how it feels. You're playing the game of society, and that's OK. Do what you need to do. Just remember, there will be better days ahead.

- **If time is a barrier, look at how you could carve out some moments for yourself.** It could be very small things, as not all of us are blessed with lots of free time. Perhaps you love the feeling of being in a warm bed while listening to the pouring of rain outside, or maybe you enjoy sinking into a bath filled with scented bubbles. I love both of these. You may not if you're a summer person or just for other reasons – you do you. Find the little things that you can fit in.

- **Obviously I will always highly recommend baking**, though I am biased! But there are so many hobbies that give you the same joy – gardening (I've got into this one lately), pottery, DIY projects, sewing, knitting, cooking, painting by numbers, music, lots more.

- **You don't have to feel creative to feel childlike.** Firstly, creativity doesn't just look like pottery, art or physically creating something. My partner Nabil isn't keen on any of those things; he doesn't want to go pottery painting with me. His creativity is in business – problem solving, coming up with creative solutions and managing people. Maths and problem solving is creativity. Research is creativity. Any time you're asking questions and figuring out solutions is creativity. You don't even have to do *any* of the above! Just make mistakes and stay curious.

- **Maybe you used to enjoy making forts out of sofa cushions or old cardboard boxes?** Gather all the pillows and blankets in your house and make an enormous pillow fort. Get your favourite snacks, turn on a good film (bonus points if it's a childhood fave) and snuggle down in your fort to watch.

- **Find ways to express yourself that don't make you feel too self-conscious**. This could look like finding ways to bring playful motifs into your home through interior design. My home is filled with plants, novelty lighting, colourful pictures and fabrics and objects that make me feel happy and playful whenever I see them. It doesn't have to be impractical, either – your home can be playful and functional at the same time. My favourite thing about interior design is the flow of rooms and space. It makes you feel at ease without fully knowing why. Nor does it have to be colourful – just let it express you (if you want to). Similarly, you could do this with your clothing.

- If you were one of those children who was never still and used to love running around, clambering about and skipping, **you could try to find more opportunities in your life for movement**. An obvious choice would be dancing, although not everyone is comfortable dancing in public. If you're not sure about that (I am not really a public dancer, unless there's some kind of repetitive beat involved, such as with rave music), try putting on your favourite song next time you're home alone and enjoy a one-person dance-fest. Or you could even go rock climbing or skydiving (you guys are bonkers and I love that for you).

- If you used to enjoy caring for your toys – perhaps combing your dolls' hair or painting miniature figures – **you might find that taking care of plants brings back some of those feelings of satisfaction**. Every time you see a new leaf forming or notice that your plant is looking green and healthy, you can enjoy that moment.

● **Bring back that curiosity!** I love to see it! As discussed, many children are told off for asking too many questions, but that's often because adults are feeling stressed or too busy – or because they don't know the answers. Children can sometimes ask questions in a way that seems rude, but after all, they *are* children. As adults, we have more knowledge and self-awareness, which lets us know how to ask questions in a more thoughtful and considered way, allowing us to express our curiosity kindly and gently. We are never too old to learn something new, so get asking those questions, however random they may be! If you don't want to ask people, search the internet. That's what I do. My internet history is embarrassing because I search so many questions. Most recently it has been 'why is Coca-Cola black?', 'Are cats trying to protect us?' (I ask a lot of cat-related questions), 'what are people with orange energy like?', what percentage of your total energy does your brain use?' (20% apparently – it's a powerful thing so we need to look after it), 'why is my pee bright yellow?' (and before you ask, there's nothing wrong with me – the answer is because I'm taking vitamin B2!). And that's not even touching on my hours spent on real estate sites looking at peoples' houses and speculating about their lives, like they're dollhouses or something. Curiosity takes many forms (and it ties into creativity a lot) – questions, making mistakes and learning from them, problem-solving, snooping on peoples' home layouts and décor...

However you decide to bring in these little moments of childlike joy, I think a key part of it is to stop to notice little moments that make you feel curious and excited, whether that's a new leaf on a plant, an unusual cloud in the sky, or a person on a train wearing a pink-and-green fluffy coat. Kids are so good at noticing and enjoying little moments – we can all learn a lot from them.

8

I'd rather be kind than pretty

'Kim-Joy is one odd-looking creature.'

'Kim-Joy looks like a clown that's been microwaved.'

'Talk about punchable faces.'

Filming *The Great British Bake Off* had had its stressful moments, but the focus of the show was the baking. Not on how I looked. As such, I hadn't thought much about my appearance – I was more interested in how my bakes looked and tasted.

Filming was long since over, but now, a day or two before the first episode was due to be broadcast, the names and photographs of the contestants had been released – and the screen in front of me was filled with cruel comments about the way I looked. Dozens of people – people who didn't know me, who had never met me – commenting so harshly on my appearance. It felt so strange.

It was a jolt to me, and I barely slept that night. Although I gradually started to get over the nasty shock, as the show began and people started watching, the comments kept coming.

'Kim-Joy is a good baker but her face is excruciating to look at.'

'Does Kim-Joy own make-up or just a box of crayons?'

'Kim-Joy is a weird-looking lassie.'

Some people even tagged me in their comments; others used the #GBBO hashtag. People always say, 'Don't read the comments,' but it was hard not to. In the end, I stopped looking at certain (more negative) social-media platforms altogether. One of my friends looked at them for me after each episode was aired, and gave me a run-down so I knew how people were reacting – they would tell me about all the positive comments, and then some negative comments so that we could laugh them off together.

Before taking part, all the contestants had met with a psychotherapist and a team who had helped us prepare for the experience of being on the show and dealing with the publicity that would come afterwards. But truthfully, however much they tried to prepare us in theory, nothing can really prepare you for what it's like in practice.

Kim-Joy is one odd-looking creature.

Talk about punchable faces.

Kim-Joy looks like a clown that's been microwaved.

Kim-Joy is a weird-looking lassie.

Does Kim-Joy own make-up or just a box of crayons?

Kim-Joy is a good baker but her face is excruciating to look at.

It took me a long time to process my feelings about these comments. I didn't just 'not care' straight away. I'd always taken pride in looking unique, but of course I'd never been bombarded by other people's inner thoughts about it either. Because often that's what these comments were: things they wouldn't dream of saying to my face, but felt comfortable typing anonymously behind the safety of a screen. They even used it as a way of bonding with other people, sharing jokes with fellow internet users about my make-up or the way my face looked.

As the later episodes aired, people seemed to like me more; perhaps it was because they'd had a chance to get to know me better, and were no longer just judging me on my appearance – but there were still some who were eager to criticize.

For a long time, I didn't do or say anything about this. A lot of people advised me to ignore the cruel comments, to 'rise above it'; but I realized that although that might be the right course of action for some people, it wasn't the right thing for me. Trying to ignore it meant the pressure was on *me* to react in the 'right' way, to pretend I was OK with it when I wasn't. My feelings were invisible, theirs were visible. Gradually, my perspective shifted. I thought, **Why not talk about it? I have a voice.** So, a few years after all this happened, I shared a series of screenshots of some of these comments on my Instagram page. For me, publicly sharing these comments on my own platform, with the warm, supportive and vibrant community I feel so lucky to have around me, took the power away from the people who had made them. The comments were no longer something I had to hold inside, making me feel bad about myself. It felt cathartic to release them into the world. It felt similar to back when the show was airing and my friend used to go through some of the mean comments with me, and we'd laugh at how ridiculously sad they were.

I wasn't engaging with the people who had been unkind (or 'feeding the trolls', as we often put it). I wasn't responding to them or answering their cruel comments. I was just sharing them. By grouping them together, I took away their unkind power and showed them for what they were: cowardly, thoughtless remarks, made by people who didn't know me at all.

My appearance is the least interesting thing about me

My experience might have been particularly public, but we all know what it's like being made to feel less-than for our appearance – perhaps some more than others, but it's still so sadly, joylessly common.

Although this can be deeply upsetting, I also think it's a bit boring when people insist on commenting on other people's looks, instead of on other things about them. Whether others like my looks or not, I'm confident that I have both talent and kindness – and I'm proud of that. Even though I enjoy playing with quirky fashion choices and colourful make-up, my appearance is the least interesting thing about me. The most interesting things are my thoughts, my personality, my kindness (again!), my love of learning and my skills. Not only are these the most interesting things about me, but they're also the things I love the most about myself.

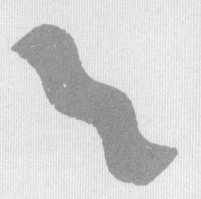

We're not always comfortable naming the things we like about ourselves, but it can be a powerful way to counteract the self-doubt and sadness that can creep in when we focus so much on outward appearance.

If it helps you, try listing five things you like about yourself. They don't have to be about your appearance, but they can be. It's OK if you struggle to think of any. If that's the case, maybe ask a loved one what they think. It's sometimes hard to believe what people say, but try to cast those cobwebs of doubt away.

Here are mine:

- I love my fashion sense and the way that I use my clothes to express myself.

- I like my hair and my glasses.

- I like how kind I am.

- I like how ambitious I am.

- I like how good I am at being comfortable.

- And I love and take pride in my unique appearance.

Your turn.

Skin deep

Unfortunately, our culture tends to equate physical beauty with being morally good, kind, intelligent and brave. In the eighteenth and nineteenth centuries, the study of physiognomy was based on the idea that how a person looked reflected their morals. It was also centred on white beauty standards. The theory was that criminals had heavy jaws, strong cheekbones and asymmetrical faces. Though physiognomy has now been debunked as a pseudoscience, these beliefs still linger in our culture and minds – sometimes consciously, but often unconsciously. **We often experience a sort of 'halo effect'**, where someone's actions are perceived in a particular way because of the way they look.

The idea that physical beauty is linked with goodness is enforced from an early age, with our favourite childhood stories and films showing us heroes who are considered good-looking, and villains who are shown to be conventionally unattractive and visibly different.

Villains are often portrayed as having 'ugly' faces, bigger noses, smaller eyes, blemishes and scars. Their bodies are malnourished or overweight, such as that of Ursula in Disney's *The Little Mermaid*. Just look at *Aladdin*: the villain, Jafar, is portrayed with a hooked nose and a long face, in contrast to Aladdin, our hero, who has big eyes and a softer, kinder-looking face. This extends even to animals. In *The Lion King*, Scar literally has a scar across his face, while his henchmen, the hyenas, are hunchbacked, bony, mangy, yellow-eyed villains. (This prejudice even sadly extends to real life – people are more likely to adopt cats and dogs that are more conventionally cute, while animals that don't fit this mould find it harder to secure a forever home.)

Of course, there are some media and films that challenge this perception; for example, *The Elephant Man*, which highlights the chasm between the way people react to the main character's physical appearance and his beautiful personality. One of my favourite films is the bittersweet stop-motion animation *Mary and Max*, in which both the main characters are isolated and struggle, partly due to their looks. Mary is bullied for a birthmark on her head, and for using clothes pegs instead of buttons. Max, who is diabetic, obsessed with chocolate hotdogs and morbidly obese, becomes agoraphobic. Both characters have other mental illnesses and difficulties, so their physical appearances are not the only reasons they struggle. They are both kind, imperfect (like all of us) and empathetic people, and form a beautiful bond.

Sadly, these more nuanced media portrayals are the minority, so we have to ensure that we are aware of and notice these biases where they arise, as our unconscious views do influence our actions and beliefs about people, whether we realize it or not. **Admitting this doesn't make us judgemental people; it makes us reflective and thoughtful.** Just like implicit racial bias is real, so is implicit beauty bias. Without being aware of its existence, unknowingly biased thoughts and actions can't be challenged.

For the joy of it

We all experience pressure to look a certain way. For example, workplaces view certain appearances as more professional, so promotions or more opportunities might be awarded to those who look a particular way, rather than being based purely on merit. Generally speaking, there is a particular pressure on women to be beautiful, to wear make-up and 'flattering' clothes, and to fit certain beauty standards that are often narrow and unattainable. Of course, society also puts pressure on men, though it's in a very different way compared to women.

Unfortunately, all of this means we live in a world where it probably isn't realistic to simply say, 'Let's just not care about how we look.' Realistically, **'pretty privilege' does exist** (although I'll come back to that in a moment as it's not entirely straightforward), and by meeting the standards that society sets for what is 'attractive', we can experience certain advantages. For example, a doctor who meets beauty standards is believed to be more trustworthy and skilled. They may find it easier to get jobs.

While I do wear make-up and curate my appearance to a certain extent to have a step up in life and 'play the game', I also like to use make-up, clothes and fashion to challenge perceptions as much as I possibly can. I choose make-up that's as fun and glittery as possible to challenge typical beauty standards, and, as we discussed in the last chapter, I wear clothes that fill my world with colour and joy.

Though it's well-meaning and I like people being nice in general, being told my make-up or clothes are 'flattering' is not my favourite compliment. For me, this kind of comment implies that I have styled my body for other people's consumption and my value lies in my ability to conform to beauty standards. I am much more comfortable with being told that my clothes, make-up and glasses are fun, or magical or look cozy. But at the same time, any compliment is nice and makes me smile!

I love fashion and it's a big interest of mine. I know it's not as simple as flipping a switch and having a whole new perspective, but I do try to make my appearance simply what *I* enjoy, rather than worrying about what others think. This is different for everyone. **You do you**.

Expressing yourself through your clothing doesn't have to be about looking appealing to someone else. Celebrating your appearance can be a way to challenge the stereotypes and embrace your own unique self. It's not about how you look, it's about what you're expressing.

But then again, this isn't every day. Some days, yes, I want to rebel against beauty standards. But other days, I want to feel beautiful within them. Most days I feel like both at the same time. I'm not constantly challenging the ideal because that takes energy and makes me worry, and some days there just isn't the energy or mental capacity, and that's OK. On those days, if I need uplifting, I look to other people for inspiration and comfort.

There's a woman who lives in Brooklyn, New York, whom I look up to as a shining example of someone who challenges conventional standards of beauty. She is often referred to as the Green Lady of Brooklyn. She is in her eighties, and, as her moniker suggests, she wears only green. Her coats, dresses and accessories are in shimmering shades of emerald, lime and chartreuse – even her hair is green. She brings smiles to everyone's faces when they meet her, and people love to take photos of her as she spreads her message of love and joy. She is my inspiration!

As I'm sure this book has made clear by now, joy is deeply important to me. I love that it is part of my name (one of the best things my parents chose for me!). Perhaps this is a form of magical thinking, but I like to think that my name has shaped my identity and goals. Joy is what I want to spread through my baking, and through the way I dress and move through the world. Joy is what I hope to share through being kind and not expecting anything in return, and through hopefully making people smile. I want to think back on my life and see the kindness and joy that I've brought to myself and others; and if I do that, I don't think I'll be worrying much about what somebody on social media thinks about the way my face looks. **The joyful moments we look back on are the things we remember** and the things that bring a twinkle to our eyes, not how stereotypically beautiful our outward appearance has been at any given moment.

A note on 'pretty privilege'

I mentioned 'pretty privilege' earlier. While it *is* a thing, it isn't a straightforward thing! Like so much in life, it's deeply nuanced. People who are conventionally attractive might enjoy many benefits as a result, but they can also experience many unwanted consequences. There can be a pressure to 'keep up appearances' and always look a certain way. They may feel under scrutiny or less valued if any part of their appearance changes. Other people might make assumptions about their intelligence or personality based on the way they look. People might dismiss their skills and assume they've only achieved the things they have because they're beautiful. They might be sexualized or taken less seriously.

Regardless of what we look like, any over-emphasis on our physical appearance is an issue for all of us.

THE HALO EFFECT

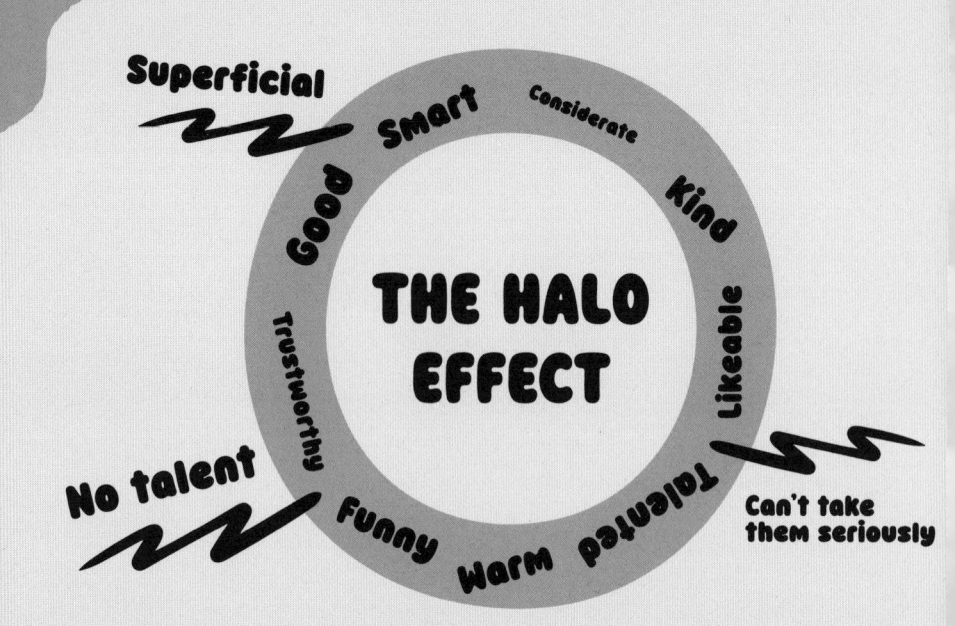

Superficial · Good · Smart · Considerate · Kind · Likeable · Can't take them seriously · Talented · Warm · Funny · Trustworthy · No talent

Challenging the narrative

Conventional beauty standards might be deeply entrenched, **but we can challenge them**. This is not to say that I expect you to love yourself unconditionally and experience total body positivity (although if you do, that's just wonderful). The truth is, this can be unrealistic for some of us. I don't totally love myself; I don't have total body positivity. Some days I feel good, and some days I feel worse and wish I looked like other people. I still have a way to go, I always will do, and that's OK. I think it's more realistic to aim for acceptance, to learn to hold yourself in positive regard, and to notice and gently challenge the moments where you are criticizing yourself for not fitting in with conventional beauty standards that don't matter to you. And if after considering everything, you still want to change your appearance to fit more with beauty standards? I get it and I'm rooting for you. It's your body, and ultimately it's your decision.

Here are some prompts that could help shift you towards enjoying your own appearance and away from outward validation and comparison. You can use these as journal prompts, things to meditate on, or discuss with a loved one.

- What are your own implicit beliefs about beauty? These might be internalized ideas that you only apply to your view of yourself, but wouldn't dream of applying to others.

- Can you think of any inspiring people (such as the Green Lady of Brooklyn) who do their own thing and celebrate their own appearance in a way that's different to the norm?

- Next time you're in a busy place, look around and notice the diversity in the way that everyone around you looks. Isn't it so much more fun and delightful that we're all so different?

- What are some ways in which you could realistically challenge conventional beauty standards? Even if they're not things you can feasibly do for yourself (which is totally OK), they could be ways of acting towards others, such as making an effort to give people compliments that aren't centred on them looking good for others, but instead focus on the joy they are giving themselves.

- Stay aware of societal views about beauty when reading books, watching films, using social media and reading the news. Notice when these implicit views and biases are impacting the way you are reacting to someone or something. This takes a lot of effort, and it's not always possible. It's something I try to do, sometimes well, and other times not so well.

Cognitive distortions

Cognitive distortions are ideas that affect the way we see things. It's like looking in a fun-house mirror and seeing a warped reflection looking back at you – but in the fun house, at least you *know* the mirror is warped. Pay attention to these distortions when they come up for you. Here are some of the most common ones that affect body image.

Black-and-white thinking

Thoughts like: *I can only be attractive if I look perfect*. This kind of attitude means we are never happy with how we look, because we only see the perceived flaws.

Comparison

Thoughts like: *I wish I had their hair/height/figure/teeth/etc*. Comparing yourself negatively to other people is a tough habit to break, but doing so means you are always dissatisfied. As a 5'9" woman, I love my height now, but as a teenager I hated how I stood out as the second tallest in my year. I wanted to be like the other girls who were petite and 'cute'. Not any more though, because being tall is very cool – and very useful.

Perhaps you look at a photo of you and a friend, and instead of seeing your happy faces, you think, *I wish I had a perfect nose like her*. Could this thought change to something else, such as *I might not love my nose, but I love that I'm such a good friend*, or *My nose looks like my mum's, and I love her for who she is, so why not myself?*

Emotional reasoning

Thoughts like: *I feel sad today, so I feel like I don't look good.* I struggle with this one when I am in a low mood. It's like everything is gloomy, and I feel like I don't look sparkly and that other people won't see me as kind because I don't look like me any more. Deep down, I know that isn't true, and that I still look the same, but it's hard to shake. I try to remind myself that on another day, I'll feel different; that this will pass.

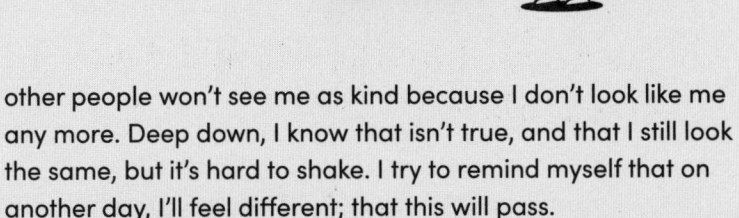

Over-generalization
Thoughts like: *That picture of me looks so bad; I must look like that all the time.* This is a form of catastrophizing, and it's not true: a photo is just a snapshot in time. It doesn't reflect your whole self. And maybe that moment is a second in time where you're happy or proud of yourself. Maybe you're graduating, maybe you're celebrating a birthday, maybe you're just enjoying the sand and sea on the beach. Recently, I met a new friend who has a cat called Sigrid who loves to ride around London with him on his bike, and he took a very cute picture of me just as Sigrid chose to sit on my lap while we were at a café. My first thought when I looked at the picture was that I had a tummy roll and maybe I should delete it. But I sat with that thought, and eventually dismissed it, because it was a wonderful moment that I wanted to remember, and that's what was most important.

Mind-reading
Thoughts like: *Everyone at the gym is looking at me. They're judging me for my size.* You don't know what anyone else is thinking. And if they are judging you (some people project their issues), that's their problem, not yours. I believe that most people are good and kind – most people are on your side. And most people are more busy feeling self-conscious about themselves than worrying about what anyone else looks like.

That picture of me looks so bad; I must look like that all the time.

I wish I was their height

I can only be attractive if I look perfect.

I feel sad today, so I feel like I don't look good.

They're judging me for my size

Acceptance

Sometimes, the more you try to make negative thoughts and emotions go away, the more you get stuck in them. Like trying to catch a fly buzzing around your house – the more you try to catch it, the more frustrated you become. Instead of trying to force that negative thought to be positive (or running around after that fly with a glass and a piece of paper), you can try to switch from your 'thinking' brain to your 'observing' brain.

The thinking brain is thinking all your thoughts and feeling all your feelings. The observing brain looks down and watches all your thoughts swim around – I imagine it to be floating somewhere on top of my head.

So, try to switch to your 'observing brain' instead of being in your thinking brain. It's not easy to do – I often switch back and forth. Then, try to identify the thought. I like to call those thoughts my 'squeaky thoughts' because I imagine them squeaking somehow. But you can called them 'tales' or 'stories' or anything you find helpful. For example, here's my 'I'm too ugly-looking' squeaky thought.

Giving them your own personal name (it can be something funny or ridiculous) helps to create distance from them. In doing so, you can start to figure out how and why your brain is coming up with these stories. For example, **Maybe it's trying to look after me by keeping me alert, in case other people target me for this.** Or, **Maybe it's replaying this story because it's linked to previous hurtful experiences.**

Then, sit back and acknowledge that the thoughts are there. You know what your brain is saying and trying to do.

Then take yourself back into present moment. Check on how your body is feeling physically. Are you holding any tension? How are you feeling? Take some time to observe what's around you. What can you see? What can you touch/hear/smell/taste? Press a part of you firmly on the ground and feel the connection, or hold an object that feels grounding and reassuring. Breathe deeply, from your abdomen. And then my favourite thing, distraction. Distract yourself with a game, some exercise, anything. For me it would be baking, playing a game or thinking about rearranging things in my home.

The thoughts are still there, but this helps you to observe them from a distance and be more compassionate to yourself. The thoughts often come back, and that's okay. The goal isn't to get rid of them, but to accept them as part of you, and in doing so, accept yourself, with all your negative thoughts and imperfections.

You can combine some of this strategy with trying to tackle your cognitive biases. On the surface, these might seem like opposite ways of dealing with things, but challenging cognitive biases doesn't mean believing that you HAVE to change this thought into something positive. It's much more gentle where you make small steps at a time, chipping away at thoughts rather than aiming to stamp them out. And again, being able to tackle the thoughts comes from your observing brain, looking down. However, if you're finding you're getting stuck in more intense thought loops where the same thoughts keep obsessively replaying for days/weeks/ longer, it can sometimes be best to observe and acknowledge the thought, then distract. Sometimes over-analyzing within these thought loops doesn't get you anywhere.

> **Note**
> If you have very intense, looping thoughts that are intrusive, and you gain temporary relief through rituals (these can be verbal, physical, or thought rituals), but no matter what you do the same thoughts still come back, then it could be worth looking into OCD.

What to do

We all experience these things differently, but for me, talking about these things really helped. Publicly putting those cruel comments out there that were fuelling negative beliefs about my own body image on social media made me put them into perspective. Sometimes, keeping thoughts quiet gives them more power. Sharing them can be powerful. If you think that could be true for you, you could consider seeking therapy or asking for support from friends or family to help you talk about your body image.

Another great thing to try is to practise more self-compassion. This is something that can help with all areas of your life, not just body image. Perhaps you can remind yourself of all the strengths and skills you have that go beyond physical appearance, and maybe you could even turn them into affirmations.

For example:

- *I'm a kind/thoughtful/diligent/creative person.*

- *I don't need to look a certain way for other people.*

- *My appearance is not for other people to consume – it's for me.*

- *I might not love every bit of my body, but I'm grateful for it.*

I may not be everyone's idea of 'pretty' or 'good looking', but I am:

- Pretty ambitious

- Pretty kind

- Pretty free

- Pretty talented

- Pretty empathetic

- Pretty loved

- Pretty loving

- Pretty brilliant

- Pretty inspiring

This last exercise can be really impactful.

I try to be grateful that I'm existing. OK, maybe I don't look the way I idealize, but I'm touching the ground. I'm connected. I'm here. I look around and know that I'm in a world that blows my mind basically every day. We live in a world where an oak tree can live to a thousand years old. Isn't that incredible? And I get to be there touching it? And I bet no one compares its wonky branches to the other trees in the forest.

9

Understanding how other people think

I was looking for a temporary Christmas job to earn some money while I was at university. I'd applied for jobs before without much success, but I was hopeful about this one: a shop assistant's role in a store that specialized in toys and games for young children. I filled out my application by hand, and when I went in for my interview, the two interviewers I spoke to marvelled at it: they'd thought it was typed.

However impressed they were with my neat handwriting, they seemed less impressed with me. At the end of the interview, one of them looked at me with a knowing smile and said, 'Maybe you would be a better fit in our Bath store – they're more... Well, they'll like you more.'

I left the interview feeling confused. What did she mean, 'they'll like you more'? Did that mean these interviewers didn't like me? That familiar feeling of not fitting in, of not being 'right', settled over me. I wondered what I had said or done in the interview to make them react like this.

And then I realized. It wasn't about me, and what I had or hadn't said or done. It was about them.

Well, I didn't fully realize then and there. It took me time and reflecting back on the experience.

People don't always give you opportunities in life based on your skills and abilities. They often focus instead on how they *feel* about you – the assumptions they make about you, often within moments of meeting you, and whether or not they feel they can relate to you. They might be wondering whether they'd be able to have a laugh with you, or whether you fit in with their expectations and assumptions around how you should look (see chapter eight).

Although I no longer had selective mutism by this stage, I was still quiet, and my social anxiety meant I could come across as very serious, despite this not being exactly how I was feeling inside. During that interview, although I hadn't said or done anything wrong in terms of my answers to the questions, the interviewers had made the decision that I wasn't 'like them', that I wouldn't fit in with the way they liked their store to be. Perhaps without realizing it, they'd already put me in the 'outsider' box.

There will always be people who misunderstand or dislike you. You could be the sweetest, plumpest and juiciest blueberry in the carton, and still some people wouldn't like you, because they just don't like blueberries. Understanding this helps me to navigate these weird grey area situations without getting lost in too many negative feelings or letting self-doubt or other people's opinions insidiously seep into my mind and distort how I actually feel about myself. I hope it helps you too.

Other people's opinions

The power of an umbrella

Other people might look at your appearance, or your behaviour, and think they know something about you. But unless they *do* know you well, the likelihood is that they've formed their opinions of you based on not very much. These assumptions are likely to come from their own cognitive biases, and therefore to have far more to do with them than with you.

Knowing that many people make assumptions about others is not about being negative or having a gloomy outlook that will keep you stuck in life – it's power. It allows you to figure out the gaps in which you CAN realistically shine and be more YOU, while also giving you the context and space to understand that other people's opinions will impact their behaviour and can consequently have an impact on you, but they are still only opinions. They aren't necessarily true; you can disagree with them. You don't have to let them become part of your identity.

I like to think of other people's opinions as being like rain drops. You can see them and hear them, but you can put up an umbrella and stop them from completely drenching you. Some opinions might be like a light drizzle that's fairly easy to shake off; others might be more like hail or even snow, or torrential rain that feels completely overwhelming. Some spray from the rain may blow into you from the side, unprotected by the umbrella, and you will almost certainly step in a puddle here and there, but by using your umbrella (your experiences, and your knowledge and understanding of how we all think), you can keep the worst of the rain away, acknowledging that it's there without getting soaked through.

Of course, you might get caught without an umbrella sometimes – it happens to all of us – but you can go home and get warm and dry. We all have our own methods for drying off after an unwelcome cloudburst of other people's opinions. Here are some ideas; think about some of your own, too.

- Talk to a friend or loved one (see chapter two)

- Write in your journal

- Make yourself comfortable and cozy

- Do something simple to bring you joy, like making a cup of tea or baking (bring in that childlike joy from chapter seven!)

- Remind yourself of everything that is good about you

Don't take them with you

Another analogy I find really useful here is to imagine that opinions are like glasses. Imagine you're moving through a crowded bar or restaurant, carrying a tray. You're trying to keep the tray balanced and make sure you don't drop anything, but as you make your way across the room, people keep putting their glasses on your tray. If you try to carry all these glasses with you, your tray will become unbearably full. It might get too heavy for you to lift; you might find that you can't even move forward anymore, because you're carrying too much. You might look at the tray and not even be able to tell which of the glasses on it were yours in the first place, and which belong to other people.

It's OK to put some of the glasses down. Other people can pick them up and carry them if they want, but they can't force you to take them.

Think about your tray. Which of the glasses you're carrying are your own beliefs and feelings about yourself – and which of them actually belong to other people? Other people's perceptions of us can end up shaping us. For example, if other people expect you to be quiet, you might feel like you can't share your opinions, because you're so aware of their expectations. I mention this example because this is something that affected me for a long time. Though now I have perhaps become the opposite in terms of sharing my opinions, and I love that because it's more of the real me. Take a look at some of the glasses you're carrying, and ask yourself:

- Is this opinion based on a judgement made by someone else?

- If so, does it tie in with how I see myself?

- If not, why am I still carrying it?

Identifying which glasses really belong on your tray can be hard. As always, there's a grey area – some opinions merge with your opinions, sometimes glasses are stacked within glasses. For instance, it wasn't simply that other people saw me as socially anxious, and then I became that. I believe part of it is just the wiring of my brain. I'm already sensitive and anxious. I've always been able to separate other people's opinions about me with my own feelings towards myself, I am not just a sponge. But perhaps I am a sponge with a hardened crust – the crust is still somewhat porous and those outside opinions inevitably seep in. It takes a while to wring them out.

I actually find it more helpful to start recognizing and challenging the thoughts of other people, by turning the idea on its head and working backwards from there. I find it helpful to reflect on some assumptions that I might have made about others in the past. We all do it.

- Do you have any particular assumptions or biases that might affect how you view others? Whether it be implicit assumptions about people based on how they look, assumptions around vulnerability.

- What influences the way you react to other people?

When I started to become more aware and pay attention to my own implicit assumptions about others, it helped me to recognize when others are making assumptions about me. And from there, I can think about whether these assumptions have any real basis, and think about whether I'm internalizing any of these beliefs. I hope this helps you too.

It's worth noting here that there is some difference between the opinions formed by people who don't really know you based on brief interactions or their own biases, and observations of repeated patterns of behaviour shared with you by loved ones. I'm not saying you should never listen to the opinions of others; just consider where they're coming from and reflect on whether they feel valid to you.

As seen on TV

It can be really fascinating to look at the way that characters on TV shows and in other consumable media are loved and admired for certain behaviours that would not receive the same response from others in real life. Think about Wednesday Addams, from the *Addams Family* film and TV series, and more recently the popular show *Wednesday*. She is blunt, pessimistic and unfriendly – and obsessed with everything dark and morbid. She often comes across as rude and uncaring. Yet, while watching the show, many people admired her for – and identified with – the very same traits that would likely lead to rejection in real life, to the point that people want to dress like her and wish to be like her. But if Wednesday was a real person, she might be seen as weird, annoying and rude – and might be excluded or be bullied. Why is it that *characters* like Wednesday are idolized, but when the very same traits are found in real people, those that love the fictional character don't like the real person?

Wednesday is confident and uniquely herself. Her fictional character represents a side of ourselves that many of us wish we could express. But in real life, there are consequences to that – we don't know where our story will lead. We could end up hurt. Maybe we've ended up hurt in the past by trying to express our bluntness, for instance. But while watching the show, we are reassured in knowing that Wednesday is the main character and she's going to save the day, or at least be important to the story. The rules are different for her. So we can escape into that fantasy world and see how traits that we may not be able to safely express, can be admirable and strong – without consequences.

After I took part in *The Great British Bake Off*, a lot of people treated me differently. I know this isn't quite the same, as Wednesday is a fictional character and I am a real person (that sounds like such an odd thing to declare). I know that some of the reason people's behaviour towards me changed was also to do with the boost in self-esteem the show gave me: not just the external validation of being praised for my baking, but also the sense of pride I felt at my achievement, and the fact that I'd pushed myself and done something big. But I also noticed that some people seemed to change their opinion of me purely because I had been on TV. People who hadn't really spoken to me before were a lot more interested in me afterwards. Nabil and I knew someone who, before I went on *Bake Off*, barely ever spoke to me, and I'd had a vague sense that they didn't think I was cool or impressive enough. But once I'd done the show, suddenly this person was inviting me to dinner. The fact I'd been on TV seemed to change their assumptions about me: now, perhaps, they thought I was successful or creative or more interesting.

When people watch you on a TV show, you become a character. The storylines are centred around focusing on the parts of you that emphasize that character. These are all accurate aspects of you, but they're magnified. And I found that some of the personality traits that had previously meant I didn't always fit in were suddenly admired. Prior to the *Bake Off*, I was seen as awkward – and not in a good way. I had numerous job applications where I got through the written application, but when I had the in-person interview, I didn't get the job. This happened time and time again, not just at that toy store. But when people viewed me as a character rather than a person, that awkwardness became quirkiness; the strangeness became interesting. It was a very unusual experience. So, while I'm not a fictional character like Wednesday Addams, I just find it a very interesting phenomenon altogether. And one that hopefully helps cement the fact that **we outsiders are actually pretty amazing** – because we are the ones people want to watch on their TV and read in their books. And many people do relate to us, even though it doesn't feel like that in real life all the time.

Romanticize and imagine your life like you are in a movie. You're the main character of your story. I see it as one of those things we all do so much as children – imagine ourselves as the hero fighting a monster, or as a doll serving the best spaghetti ever. It's a nice way to bring back that inner-child joy, whilst also not taking things too seriously. Imagine yourself holding that big umbrella, and laugh at other people's opinions when you can – after all, they are often quite peculiar and illogical.

Finding your favourites
I am also very happy to say that a lot of people *didn't* change their behaviour towards me. It didn't matter to them whether I'd been on TV or not. People like this have always been my favourites.

I think this just goes to show that the right people for you will like you for who you are. That might sound like a cliché, but it's often true. And those people *are* out there; you just need to find them, and not let the rest bother you. This is easier in theory than in practice, but knowledge is power, and understanding these things can help you to feel happier within yourself. Put up your umbrella, check your tray for excess glasses, and pay attention to the people who are right for you.

For me, these were people who just 'got' me; who would rather go to a board game night than the pub, who loved the same comics and films and shared the same interests. Perhaps you'll find your people at a book club, or a punk show, or in an online community. Perhaps you've already found them. Keep an eye out for those people who are like genuine rays of light shining on you, peeking through the storm clouds.

Cognitive dissonance and cognitive bias

Despite my enthusiasm for finding your people (and I really do think it can be life-changing), the fact is, everyone experiences the world differently. Just as we generally socialize with people who are similar to us, we also generally seek out and prioritize information that confirms our prior beliefs. We develop a schema throughout our lives, and everything we experience is interpreted through that lens. The best way to challenge this schema in ourselves is to be aware of it and actively reflect on it. Not everyone around you will take this approach, so try your best not to put energy into them, if you can help it. Sometimes, of course, it is beneficial to try to challenge the views of those you strongly disagree with, because in order for there to be change, we have to engage with people who think differently to us, and to speak out against prejudiced views. **But you also have to pick your battles**, and your own energy and mental health should come first.

When other people challenge us because they believe our opinions are wrong, or that we have experienced a certain event differently to them, it can be hard to navigate. Remember that gym instructor who made me feel so uncomfortable that I walked out of his class (see page 30)? Well, as I explained, when I got home, once I'd had a chance to absorb how I felt about it all, I shared my experience on social media. I want to be really clear here: I didn't name the instructor or the gym; I wasn't trying to shame anyone or get anybody in trouble. I was sharing my experience, and also the fact that, despite being upset, I was proud of myself for walking away from a situation that was uncomfortable for me.

Soon after, I received a message from someone I'd never met before. It turned out that this person had been in the gym class and witnessed the whole thing, but they felt I'd completely misunderstood the situation. The whole thing was only a joke, they told me. The gym instructor had been messing about, and I was the only who'd been bothered by it. The instructor was, they said, a great person, who had helped them lose weight and grow in confidence. They went on to tell me that the reason I was upset was because I wasn't confident in myself and had a victim complex, thinking everyone else was out to get me.

This struck me as really interesting; this person and I had both had very different experiences of the same instructor. I didn't doubt what they were saying about how positively the instructor had impacted their life – but that didn't mean my experience hadn't happened. **Both our experiences could be true and exist together in the same universe.** But the person writing the message didn't share this attitude: they felt that I was just plain wrong, and they wanted to tell me so.

I can't be sure, of course, but my gut feeling was that two things had come into play when they felt the overwhelming urge to send me an essay about all this.

- **A preconceived belief that tears and vulnerability are weakness.** A belief that crying or showing vulnerability indicates you are not confident in yourself, and that you see yourself as a victim, rather than being someone who is strong and able to 'take a joke'.

- **Cognitive dissonance.** This is a really interesting one. Cognitive dissonance is the unease felt when your own actions, or those of someone else towards whom you feel positive, don't align with your values or beliefs. It can also be entirely internal – where you are holding two opposing views at once.

There are numerous ways in which cognitive dissonance can play out, but one example is that when people have a bond with someone, and have positive feelings towards them, it can mean they struggle to deal with or accept the opposing information that this person can also be imperfect. It's two conflicting viewpoints.

None of us are perfect at letting go of cognitive dissonance – I'm definitely not – but it's a useful thing to reflect on in this sort of situation. For instance, I know my partner Nabil is the most generous person I know, and I will certainly stick up for him and his kind intentions – but I also acknowledge that if someone else is upset by his actions, then they have the right to feel that way. **Nobody is perfect: we're not just good or bad**. Even the kindest among us will sometimes do things that don't align with their usual behaviour.

As I said, I have no way of knowing whether this is why this person sent me a message. These are just potential theories that helped me to think the situation through. I could be completely wrong. But it's still useful to be aware of possible reasons for other people's behaviour, because it helps bolster your belief in yourself and not hold on to external opinions.

Choose your battles

I mentioned earlier that it's important to choose your battles when it comes to dealing with other people's opinions – but I confess that due to my own obsessive nature and thought loops, I did end up responding to this person. I wrote a (polite) essay of my own in response, and put time and energy into replying to them, because my own schema and core beliefs about myself include the feeling that I'm often misunderstood, and that to be misunderstood is catastrophically bad, and so I have to correct this somehow, even if it's a stranger. They never responded to my message.

Looking back, it would have been better for me just to talk to a friend about it all, maybe try to have a laugh, then play some board games instead. This in itself takes effort: trying to come to terms with the idea that sometimes, people are going to misunderstand me; they are going to think something of me that I disagree with or know is not true; they are going to jump to conclusions. **Sometimes, these battles are just not worth it**. Sometimes, people don't want to or don't have the energy to commit to understanding you – and you can't make them. What you can do is commit to understanding yourself and try to apply your knowledge to help you better understand others.

A last note

Despite the experiences we all sometimes have with people who make assumptions about us or have opinions that don't align with ours, it's important to remember that **generally people are good and kind, and they want to be good and kind**. Understanding that we are all biased in our thinking doesn't take away from that; it gives you the power to recognize what's going on rather than feeling hurt or under attack. We're more united than not, and have a lot in common that brings us together, even when we seem to be very different. Knowing yourself and knowing others is not about being cynical or judging other people for the way they think. It allows you to take joy and comfort in the fact that most of the time, everyone is just doing their best.

Conclusion

On these pages you will find summaries of the messages and takeaways from all the chapters in this book.

Some people won't like you, and it's OK to say no

We all have core beliefs about ourselves, which often stem from repeated messages during our childhoods. These can be positive, but it's usually the negative ones that stick around.

Certain negative core beliefs can lead to ignoring or rejecting your own wants and needs, and prioritizing those of others.

Standing up for yourself isn't always easy – it's OK (and freeing!) to acknowledge the barriers to doing this, so you can focus on areas that can actually be changed.

With time and effort, you can challenge people-pleasing behaviours and say no to things that do not serve you.

Finding the people and spaces that bring you calm and joy

We don't always understand our own needs, and this can lead to decisions that aren't right for us.

Having people/spaces that make you feel safe helps give you the resources to make the gradual, joyful changes in your life that are talked about in these chapters. There is no specific method to finding your people and spaces.

You can learn to recognize the people who fill you up – and those who drain you. It's not as black and white as dividing people into 'good' and 'bad' for you. Some people are in the middle, and people change over time.

Having a space – whether that's a whole home, a bedroom or even just one corner that makes you feel safe and calm – allows you to recharge and thrive.

We all have different needs (and resources), and we all flourish under different conditions. Take the time to figure out what works – and is accessible – for you.

'Fake it till you make it' and imposter phenomenon

It's normal to question your own skills and feel anxious about work from time to time. Imposter phenomenon is when this reaches an extreme – when, despite having all the abilities and skills required for something, you feel you are a fraud.

Marginalised groups and people who struggle in general in society are hit harder by imposter phenomenon.

If you experience it, understanding the root causes (such as low self-esteem, perfectionism, adverse childhood experiences and ingrained core beliefs) can help you to challenge it and show up as you.

Too quiet

It's OK to be quiet and it's OK to be chatty. We're all different.

People often have preconceptions about being quiet but these are not grounded in reality. Being quiet isn't the same as having low self-esteem, lacking confidence or being introverted. These are all separate aspects of personality.

Just as there is strength in being talkative, there is power in being quiet.

Laziness doesn't exist

'Laziness' is a construct, and is often applied as a discriminatory label to marginalised groups, people of colour, disabled people and people facing socioeconomic disadvantages.

Everyone has different energy levels, physical abilities and time constraints. We all have different amounts of finite resources to 'spend' on different activities. These can change over time.

We are often taught that our productivity is our worth. It's good to try to challenge this message where possible, but it's not always that straightforward. Pick your battles.

Rest is not a reward, it's a need. Find out what rest looks like for you and reclaim it. You are not lazy. There's no such thing.

Vulnerability

Showing vulnerability is not weakness – it can be a strength. It takes bravery and courage.

Being authentically you means being vulnerable. It builds trust, helps others connect with you and feel safe.

Being vulnerable can be a risk, but it often leads to moments of connection and understanding.

If you are pressured into being vulnerable when you are truly not ready to do so, stick to your boundaries. Vulnerability can't be forced – it's about genuine connection and honesty.

Being childlike

We are often taught to reject 'childlike' things, but they can be a source of great joy. Why should the world be colourless and dull just because we're adults?

Embracing the things that bring you a sense of childlike joy does not mean being childish, immature or irresponsible.

Bringing a sense of play into your life can spark creativity and build connection.

There are outside factors that make embracing your childlike side easier or more difficult.

I'd rather be kind than pretty

Society tends to equate 'beauty' with 'goodness'. These standards and assumptions tend to stay with us throughout our lives and meeting the standard can bring advantages and privileges.

You may want to challenge beauty standards, whilst also wanting to meet the beauty standard. It's OK to feel ambiguous.

You don't have to fit in with others' expectations for how you should look.

The way we look is typically the least interesting thing about us.

Understanding how other people think

Knowledge is power. Understanding how other people think is important for knowing their motivations.

Most people want to be good and kind, but everyone has their own internal biases, including you! People may apply these to you. It's not necessarily because you've done something wrong – it's often about them, not you.

Other people's opinions can be helpful – but often they are not. You don't have to accept or internalize them.

It's not always worth challenging other people's assumptions about you. Understanding that they are assumptions can be enough. Do what's right for you.

The end.

...No.

I hope this message comes through throughout this book – that there is no end or specific destination labelled 'joy' or 'authenticity'. And what 'joy' looks like is different for us all.

I've certainly learnt a lot about myself through writing this. When I first started, I was very unwell with chronic migraine. Cognitive issues meant that while the thoughts buzzed intensely in my brain, I struggled to form them into coherent sentences to write down, and thinking in and of itself caused my head to throb. It felt ironic to be writing a self-help book, when I felt like I couldn't even look after myself. My publisher supported me, suggesting a co-writer (Tara O'Sullivan) to help me. I agreed. Initially it hurt my pride as I love writing – but then I talked it through with friends and recognized that there is nothing shameful about accepting help and accommodations for a disabling condition. It wasn't 'giving up'. And in hindsight? Writing this book has brought me joy in many ways.

A big reason why I studied psychology and worked in the mental health field was because helping other people also helped to bring me peace and happiness, in the same way that baking for other people is an act of self-care. Writing this book for you to read has helped me to experience more joy too.

Joy from being vulnerable. Joy from keeping my boundaries (I love to share, but not to the extent of feeling too exposed). Joy from being curious about life. Joy from quietening my feelings about being an imposter – because I went from being a mental health specialist, to a baker of all things cute, to a cookbook author and now the writer of a book called *Ordinary Joy*. I can be all of these things. Joy from reaching out to you. Joy from knowing this book won't be for everyone, and I'm OK with that. Joy from recognizing that I am always doing my best, and proud of it. Joy from embracing both my quiet and chatty sides (everyone in my life has heard a lot about every topic in this book!). Joy from having empathy. Joy from believing in you. Joy from being childlike and including little goblins in this book.

And, finally, joy from persistence and better health – because a month or so into the writing process, I finally found some medications to help with my chronic migraine. It's still a daily issue, but it's so much better.

I've shared my own personal stories to show that I am not perfect – far from it – and hopefully you can relate to some of them, though your own stories will be different from mine. One of the most joyous things is not the similarities between us, but the differences in all our experiences. I'm a big believer in the idea that the more we share our unique perspectives, the more united we feel – and the more joy we accumulate. So I hope my stories make you think about your own life, and the stories you want to create (and potentially share) in the future.

If there is one message you take with you from this book, I hope it is this: embracing and understanding your own authentic self invites space for simple, ordinary joy, every day.

Acknowledgements

Thank you to the people in my life who have guided me towards finding myself. I appreciate you all. And I'm grateful for all of you who have rooted for me and kept me moving forwards. From those of you on social media, supporting me with your likes and comments, to people I bump into who compliment my outfit, and to those random people for those little insights that have helped to change my trajectory. You're all full of joy that is both ordinary and meaningful.

Thank you also to the team at Quadrille for supporting me when my health became debilitatingly bad whilst I was writing this book. My co-writer Tara O'Sullivan has been invaluable, sorting through all my diagrams and rambles of notes and thoughts. I couldn't have done this without you, Tara.

About the author

Kim-Joy is a bestselling cookbook author, loved for her unapologetically whimsical and joyful baked creations. Prior to rising to fame on the *Great British Bake Off* 2018, Kim-Joy worked with people from all walks of life, including vulnerable people. She has degrees in Sociology (Bsc) and Psychology (Msc), is a qualified Psychological Wellbeing Practitioner and has treated patients with anxiety and depression. Kim-Joy is also a spokesperson for mental health, self-acceptance and finding joy in the everyday.

She is an ambassador for The Wren Bakery, a Leeds-based charity helping women with multiple disadvantages to gain a better future for themselves through learning baking skills.

Kim-Joy lives in Leeds, UK with her partner Nabil and her cats, Inki and Mochi.

Instagram @kimjoy
TikTok @kimjoyskitchen
YouTube @Kim-Joy